Changed Forever By His Grace

Rhonda Lea Elliott

OlivePress
צהר זית

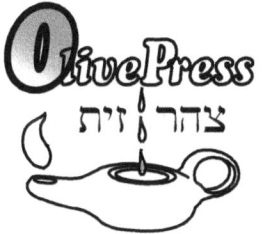

Forever Changed By His Grace

Rhonda Lea Elliott

Changed Forever By His Grace

Copyright © 2012 by Rhonda Lea Elliott

All rights reserved. No part of this book may be reproduced, stored in a retrieval system or transmitted in any way by any means—electronic, mechanical, photocopy, recording or otherwise—without the prior permission of the copyright holder, except as provided by USA copyright law.

ISBN **978-0-9855241-0-4**

1. Autobiography: ethnic 2. Messianic Judaism
3. Christian Life - Inspirational
Cover artwork, copyright © 2012 by Karen Van Lieu
created with her student, Ella Zehr
kavanlieu@gmail.com   *Karen A. Van Lieu*
                      Turin, N.Y. 13473

Cover and interior design by Cheryl Zehr, Olive Press

All Scriptures with references are taken from the New King James Version. Copyright © 1982 by Thomas Nelson, Inc. All rights reserved.

Published by
Olive Press
Messianic and Christian Publisher
www.olivepresspublisher.com
olivepressbooks@gmail.com

Messianic & Christian Publisher

Our prayer at Olive Press is that we may help make the Word of Adonai fully known, that it spread rapidly and be glorified everywhere. We hope our books help open people's eyes so they will turn from darkness to Light and from the power of the adversary to God and to trust in ישוע Yeshua (Jesus). (From II Thess. 3:1; Col. 1:25; Acts 26:18,15 NRSV *New Revised Standard Version* and CJB *Complete Jewish Bible*) May this book in particular cause hearts to more fully understand our Savior's grace..

This book is dedicated to the Lord God of Israel; the God of Abraham, Isaac and Jacob. Without His eternal, immeasurable love for me, none of this could ever have been written.

Revelation 12:11
> *And they overcame him by the blood of the Lamb and by the word of their testimony, and they did not love their lives to the death.*

John 8:32
> *And you shall know the truth, and the truth shall make you free.*

Jeremiah 29:13
> *And you will seek Me and find Me, when you search for Me with all your heart.*

Matthew 7:7
> *Ask, and it will be given to you; seek, and you will find; knock, and it will be opened to you.*

Proverbs 8:17
> *I love those who love Me, and those who seek Me diligently will find Me.*

Jesus, You Gave Me Your Life

I spent so many years
Bound up in my fears
Searching for the Truth
Pursuing You, my King
To only You I cling

You came into my heart
When we were far apart
You set me free
And gave to me
New Life,
Jesus, you gave to me Your Life

I once cried bitter tears
I once was hurt and wounded
And now I still cry tears
But they are an ointment
A sweet and simple offering
Of love returned to you from me

Jesus, how can I repay
The love you gave to me?
I just want to make each day
A sweet and simple offering

You came into my heart
When we were far apart
You set me free
And gave to me
New Life
Jesus, you gave to me Your Life.

Rhonda Lea 1992

SPECIAL THANKS to my husband John who believed in me and did not give up encouraging me to write this book. His prayers have upheld and strengthened me. He, next to Jesus, is the solid rock in my life upon whom I know I can lean on in times of trouble and sing and dance with in times of joy. Thank you, my love.

IN MEMORY OF my mother who was a poignant example to me of love and humility, the woman who put me on the path that led me to Jesus.

IN MEMORY OF my father who inspired me to dream the impossible dream and accomplish great things if I put my mind and my heart fully into it.

WITH GRATEFUL LOVE TO my two children who are God's most treasured gift to me and to my adorable grandchildren with whom God has blessed me beyond measure.

To my sister and my two brothers whose 60th birthday gift to me along with my children, made it financially possible for me to purchase my own computer and who have been asking me since I retired, "Are you writing yet?"

To all the teachers and librarians and members of this small community who told me how much they enjoyed my newspaper articles and to all the people who have come in and out of my life through the years, including friends who enrich my life; pastors and messianic rabbis who have imparted truth to me and who have been true examples of Christian love to my husband and me. You have all had a part in God's plan for us. *"For I know the thoughts that I think toward you, says the LORD, thoughts of peace and not of evil, to give you a future and a hope"* (Jeremiah 29:11).

My appreciation goes to Cheryl Zehr, Director of Olive Press and her team. Thank you, Cheryl, for working tirelessly to take my manuscript and turn it into a book to the praise and honor of the Lord.

The following is an excerpt by Shimon Peres in the Forward to *Dawn of the Promised Land*, Ben Wicks' book about the birth of the modern state of Israel.

"With echoes of the Holocaust and European persecution still ringing in their ears, these courageous pioneers *chose hope over despair*. Undaunted by a hostile landscape born of centuries of neglect, these determined adventurers chose to reclaim a land and *turn failure into great accomplishment*."

Ezekiel 37:11-14   *Then He said to me, "Son of man, these bones are the whole house of Israel. They indeed say, 'Our bones are dry, our hope is lost, and we ourselves are cut off! Therefore prophesy and say to them, 'Thus says the Lord GOD: "Behold, O My people, I will open your graves and cause you to come up from your graves, and bring you into the land of Israel. Then you shall know that I am the LORD, when I have opened your graves, O My people, and brought you up from your graves. I will put My Spirit in you, and you shall live, and I will place you in your own land. Then you shall know that I, the LORD, have spoken it and performed it," says the LORD.'"*

TABLE OF CONTENTS

SKETCHES OF MY EARLY CHILDHOOD

Chapter 1	"Why Do They Say We Killed Jesus?"	13
Chapter 2	"Oy Vey! The Children Don't Have Clothes for Such a Place!"	27
Chapter 3	"But, I Didn't Mean To!"	39
Chapter 4	"Go Fight Your Own Battles!"	51

GROWING UP

Chapter 5	"Maybe Next Year"	61
Chapter 6	"Where Do I Belong?"	69
Chapter 7	"You Don't Know Who He Is?!"	85
Chapter 8	"Don't Worry. We Can Take Care of This."	101

WANDERING, WONDERING JEW

Chapter 9	"I Could Use Some Good News!"	111
Chapter 10	"Don't You Touch That Phone!"	121
Chapter 11	"Please, God, Just Get Us Through the Night!"	129
Chapter 12	"There Has to Be a Change in My Life!"	139

FOLLOWING MESSIAH

Chapter 13	"Jesus Still Loves You."	155
Chapter 14	"The Child Came Running"	175
Chapter 15	"Lady, Take Your Chances."	191
Chapter 16	"Don't Drop the Cookies!"	225
Chapter 17	"Where's the Fire?"	239
Appendix:	Encouraging Scriptures	251
	Messianic Prophecies and Fulfillments	252

Sketches Of My Early Childhood

CHAPTER 1

"Why Do They Say We Killed Jesus?"

The delicious aroma of homemade chicken soup drifted through the air and up my nostrils causing me to daydream of sitting down to eat those plump matzo balls and soft carrots that floated in a sumptuous broth that only my mother could cook. I was jolted out of my daydream when Mummy abruptly stated half to herself, half to me, "Rhonda, I don't know why they say we killed Jesus. He was one of us. Why would we kill one of our own?"

How did my mother, a woman who had been raised in an observant Jewish home by Russian Jewish immigrants, know that Jesus was a Jew? That thought had simply not occurred to my young six year old mind. In the few years of my existence up to that moment, as far as I could remember, no one had ever told me much about Jesus. "Who was Jesus?" I asked my mother.

"I think he was a doctor because I have heard that he healed a lot of people," she replied.

I did not have the intellectual capacity to know what to do with this information but it set my heart on a journey for the next thirty years to find out who this Jesus was.

This is how it all began. On March 23, 1946, I made my arrival into this world in a small, red brick building, which was the first Mt. Sinai Hospital of Toronto. Later, my sister Gilda was born in that same hospital, as were my older brothers, Larry and Stan.

> The Toronto Hebrew Maternity and Convalescent Hospital, located in the neighborhood which is now Yorkville, was founded in 1923. The name was changed in 1924 to Mount Sinai because Jewish doctors were not allowed to intern or to hold positions in a "Toronto" hospital at that time. "Through the 1930's and 40's universities and professional schools also set quotas on Jewish enrollment or refused Jewish students completely. For example, the Toronto General Hospital accepted only one Jewish internship per year." ("Anti-Semitism in Canada," Wikipedia, the free encyclopedia.)
>
> Many Jewish people I have met in Toronto were born in the old Mount Sinai Hospital.

Chapter 1

I have been told that not too long after Gilda's birth our mother had what they called a nervous breakdown. I was just a toddler at the time. My brother Larry, a young boy of perhaps eleven years old then, was at home alone with Mother when she fell unconscious to the floor. He telephoned one of the relatives and the next thing he knew, an ambulance arrived and took his mommy away on a stretcher. She was sent to an asylum in Whitby, Ontario. When I was a young girl, my father related to me that he had insisted on taking our mother out of the hospital after she had been there for nine months. She had been refusing to eat and he was worried that his Esther might die if he didn't take action.

My two aunts cared for my sister Gil and me for a period of time while our mother was absent. After she returned home, a number of nannies were hired to care for us until Mother was able to do so herself. The only one that I remember is tall, redheaded Kay.

I was too young to know much about Kay. All I knew was that she and her young son shared a room on the second floor of our house and that she was Catholic. I was very curious about the statue of Mary over her bed. I knew it was Mary because Kay told me. She sternly instructed me never to touch the statue because Mary was the mother of Jesus. I had no idea what she meant but I was too timid to ask. Because of Kay, we switched from chicken soup on Friday evenings to fish and chips. We carried on with this tradition after Kay left us and when we were old enough, Gil and I had the task of going to the fish and chip restaurant on Avenue Road and Davenport to bring the meal home. We loved it. The hot food was wrapped in newspaper and we clutched the parcels close to our chests as we scurried home with the delicious aroma wafting up into our nostrils. That's enough about fish and chips. Now, let me tell you about my mother.

My mother's name was Esther Miriam. She was born March 11, 1907. When she was thirteen she was taken out of school to care for her six brothers and two sisters. She was the oldest of her siblings and her mother, whom we called Bubbie, was in poor health.

My first memory of Mother is when we were very little and had been playing out in the snow, sliding down an icy slope at the end of our street. Our snowsuits were soaked right through and Kay instructed my mother to discipline us because we had been told not to wander away from the house. I remember Kay physically placing my mother in a chair and holding her hand to show her how to spank us. As my little sister and I stood there, ready to take our punishment, we looked on in confusion at our mother who appeared to be in a comatose-like state. This must have taken place not too long after she came home from Whitby because that is the only time I can recall her being in such a condition.

On the contrary, I remember my mother as a warm, affectionate woman. When I was about four years old I was standing at the top of the wooden flight of stairs on the second floor of our house. The next thing I knew, I somehow tripped and fell, tumbling down to the bottom. Mummy came running and lifted me, a sobbing little girl, into her arms. I was frightened but not injured, so Mummy cuddled and rocked me back and forth, sitting on a dining room chair. I sank into her soft, cushiony arms and drifted off into a soothing, peaceful slumber. Mummy was the one who rushed to my kindergarten class to bundle me into a taxi cab and take me to Sick Children's hospital because I had broken my wrist playing "crack the whip" on the ice in the school yard. Other memories are of a tenacious woman who chased me through the house and out into the yard until she caught me so she could burst a boil on my stomach. Even though Mummy was overweight, I couldn't outrun her! I have memories of Gil (short for Gilda) and me, after misbehaving, running up the stairs at home with Mummy in hot pursuit, yelling, "When I catch you, I'm going to smack you down!" There was only one time when we thought Ma was really serious and we ran for our lives. We were sometimes very naughty, but she didn't have it in her heart to physically strike us.

Mummy seemed to be forever chasing after someone. If she wasn't running onto the verandah with Daddy's brown paper

Chapter 1

lunch bag as she hollered to him on the street, "Albert, Albert you forgot your lunch," she was running down the verandah steps after Gilda and me on our way to high school, shouting, "Rhonda, Gilda, I have scrambled eggs and toast on the table for you!"

"Sorry Ma, we're late for school," would be our quick reply as we raced along the street to catch our bus at the corner.

Often, I would dash back to the house because I had forgotten one of my school books and, as Mummy handed it to me she would say, "Rhonda, you would forget your head if it wasn't attached to your neck!"

My two older brothers, Stan and Larry, have both been a strong positive influence in my life, although I didn't see as much of Larry in my early years. He is ten years older than me and had left home by the time I was six or seven. He visited often but because of the age difference, we didn't get to know him very well until we were older. I was closer to Stan since he is only four years older than me.

Stan was the one I could talk to about my problems and know that he would really listen. He was also the one who was there for me, to dry my tears. I remember one time I was so upset about something or other that I cried until I could hardly open my eyes. Stan found me in the upstairs hallway and took me to the bathroom where he laid compresses of warm water on my eyes and talked soothingly to me until I felt better. At times such as that, Stan was like "John Boy" with his little sisters in the Walton series.

Other times he was the typical mischievous brother. One winter, our bedroom on the third floor was so cold that Gil and I kept our socks on when we went to bed. One night Stan told us, "Don't you know that potatoes will grow between your toes if you keep your socks on while you sleep?" What's incredible is that we actually believed him!

My siblings and I grew up in an area of Toronto that was called "The Annex." We lived at 73 Dupont Street which was not a Jewish neighborhood as were Kensington and Brunswick Avenues. My mother's father, Grandfather Wilson, had purchased the home for our parents. It was a red brick, semi-detached, three storey building with a narrow alley between ours and the next semi-detached home. We had a wooden verandah in the front which had a powder blue floor and steps leading up to it with a cream colored railing trimmed in green. There was a small porch off the kitchen at the back of the house where a clothes line ran along the length of the back yard to a post at the end. My brother Larry fixed a contraption on the porch ceiling with which he did pull ups. It worked fine until he pulled the roof down.

When I was about three or four years old, a photographer came to our house to take a professional photograph of the four of us children. The night before the big event, I had to endure Kay painstakingly inserting bobby pins in my hair to make it curly like my little sister's. Gil had large blue eyes and a head full of thick blonde curls. She reminded us of "Little Orphan Annie" from the popular comic strip at the time. In contrast, my hair was jet black and as straight as a board.

I was very fidgety and did not want to hold still while my hair was being worked on. I could hardly wait to get away from her because she had been drinking and her breath made me feel sick and dizzy. It seemed like she took hours. I was so relieved when she was finally finished. I slept with pin curls in my hair and the next morning, when the bobby pins were removed, I looked like a dark-haired Shirley Temple.

The photographer arrived and seated the four of us on our maroon colored sofa with the diamond patterned upholstery. Gilda and I were placed in the middle with Stan and Larry on the outside. Stan was beside me and he had quite a job to try to get me to stop crying so I would look at the camera. I was paralyzed with fear. The big black box had a curtain over it and was balanced on four thin poles. I was traumatized as I saw a man's arm sticking out the side holding a huge orange bulb attached to a rubbery hose. I wanted no part of it. I finally looked up with a sullen face

Chapter 1

long enough for the flash of blinding light and then it was over. I slid down off the sofa and scurried away as fast as my little legs would carry me.

Early one morning, about a year later, Daddy brought home a mysterious cardboard box for my sister and me, now around four and five years old, With a twinkle in his steel blue eyes and a silly grin on his face, he told us he had a big surprise. With excited anticipation we could hardly stand still in the middle of the kitchen. As I remember, it was before breakfast and we were in our pajamas. We jumped up and down in our bare feet on the cool linoleum floor while Daddy carefully put the box down and told us to open it. How delighted we were when inside we found an adorable, furry little kitten. Gil and I took turns holding and cuddling it. It was a tortoiseshell color and Daddy said he picked out a male cat because he did not want more kittens. So, we named him Tommy. But in the spring, Tommy got pregnant so we had to change his name to Teresa.

Our mother loved Teresa even though, as the cat grew, she would get under Mummy's feet in the kitchen. When we heard a screech, we knew that Mummy had accidentally stepped on Teresa's tail again. Mother sometimes even gave our cat raw eggs and fresh cooked chicken livers as a treat. She told us that it would make her fur nice and shiny. I think she was right. Our cat had the smoothest, shiniest fur that I had ever seen.

God had gifted our mother with a beautiful singing voice. "Oh Danny Boy" was one of her favorite songs, along with several Christmas carols. I therefore grew up with a love for Christmas carols. I loved hearing them on the radio or in a department store during the Christmas season. There were certain ones that moved me to tears, and still do. Three that had the most impact on my heart were "Oh Holy Night", "What Child is This?" and "O Come O Come Emmanuel." The Holy Spirit was drawing me to Jesus from a very young age.

Ma also had a favorite lullaby she would sing to us: "Here Comes the Sandman." When we were still giggling, rather than sleeping, she would exclaim loudly, "Do you want me to sing this or not!" Gil and I would then settle down and close our eyes like two little angels.

My mother had a child-like innocence and naïveté about her that defies description so that she always seemed to see the best in every situation. I still remember the twinkle in her eyes as she would sing a tune or use her incredible gift to create a new rhyme or saying to fit any occasion. On rainy days when my sister and I were bored, Mother would make fireman's hats for us out of newspaper and recite, "Rain, rain, go away, come again some other day." If we asked, "Mummy, mummy, what should we do?" Mother would reply, "Sit in a chair and fall through!" This would set us to giggling and we would quickly forget about our boredom. To make doing dishes seem like a game, she would say, "Do the dishes allowishes." Then, Gilda and I would pretend that a wicked task master was over us two little Cinderellas, until we worked faster and faster to get the job done. Our paper boy never seemed to tire of hearing Mother tell him, "You're so bright, I bet your mother calls you sunny!"

At times, I was a mischievous child. One spring when I was perhaps around six years old and my sister five, I came down with the mumps. I was in bed one afternoon when I overheard my mother's voice from downstairs, "Gilda, I tell you what. As soon as your sister is sleeping, you and I can go downtown to see a movie." Feeling left out and missing all the fun, I played a very naughty trick on my mother. With quiet determination, I slid out from under the sheets and crept stealthily into the third floor hall closet where I found my sister's spring coat and mine. I first put hers over my nightgown and then mine on top before crawling back under the blankets pretending to be fast asleep. Shortly after that I could hear Mummy looking for Gil's coat and when she came into our room she could see that I had both coats on

Chapter 1

and was sleeping like an angel. Mummy said, "Oh, poor Rhonda must be feeling chilled. We can't wake her up as she needs her rest. We will just have to go to the movies another day. It's too cold outside to go without your coat." Gil cried from the disappointment. I started to feel a little guilty, along with being terribly overheated, but I didn't have the courage to open my eyes and confess the truth.

On many a summer Sunday afternoon, Mummy took Gil and me to the Royal Ontario Museum located at Bloor Street and Avenue Road. I never ceased to be astonished and impressed with the vastness of the high domed ceilings and the immaculately polished floors. I had an irresistible urge to run and glide over the glossy surface—if I could only escape my mother's watchful eye for a moment. Gil and I never tired of asking Mummy to take us to see the Egyptian mummies. We were absolutely fascinated by them.

As we walked home downhill on Avenue Road she would exclaim, "Girls, let's have a sundae on a Sunday!" So, we would stop at the grocery store and purchase a Dixie Cup which was a small paper cup filled with ice cream. We would happily devour our ice cream with little wooden spoons as we walked home.

The second floor of our house consisted of our parents' bedroom which had a small balcony out front. Halfway down the hall was another bedroom, then a bathroom. On the other side of the bathroom there was a bedroom which my father converted into an upstairs kitchen looking out onto the backyard.

We had boarders who would rent the bedroom and kitchen on the second floor. They couldn't have had much privacy because the bathroom separated the kitchen from their bedroom and that was the only bathroom in the house. So, we usually had anywhere from six to eight people sharing the bathroom which was not unusual in those days.

Having renters gave us the opportunity to become acquainted with many unique and interesting personalities. One particular lady was from Nova Scotia. Her name was Dora and she loved baking lemon meringue pies. It seemed that she was always baking those pies and to this day, I really enjoy a good lemon meringue pie! Another renter, Bill, accidentally took a gulp of fresh warm chicken fat from a jar in our refrigerator before he realized what it was. It hadn't hardened yet and looked just like apple juice! Needless to say, he was more careful after that. My father said that if he had poured it into a glass before drinking it he would have noticed that it was fat and not juice.

One of our renters turned out to be a rather unsavory character. His name was Irving and he worked for a tabloid newspaper. Our father evicted him and as Irving was leaving the house, he started shouting obscenities at my little sister and me while we were playing with our skipping ropes on the sidewalk. He was spewing terrible accusations at our father as we stood there frightened and dumbfounded. Our big brother Larry happened to be visiting that day and he came bounding out the front door, down the steps, chasing Irving all the way to the end of the street. "Don't you dare come back! And stay away from my little sisters!" he bellowed in a voice that could be heard all the way to the Toronto Islands!

Larry was born in 1935. He had rheumatic fever when he was a small child and after he was cured, Mummy would often declare, "It was Dr. Giddens who saved your brother's life with penicillin!" There were three elementary schools in our district at the time, Huron Street School, Brown Street School, and Jesse Ketchum. Jesse Ketchum was known to be in a rough neighborhood, but more about that later. The walk to Brown Street School was uphill most of the way so Mummy chose Huron Street School because, in Larry's weakened state after his illness, the walk on level ground would be much more beneficial to his health. Naturally, the rest of us followed him there.

I have recently discovered from Larry that his bout with rheumatic fever was not his only fight for life during childhood. The most traumatic incident was when he was eight years old. He was

Chapter 1

chased by a gang of boys who shouted, "Get the Jew!" as they ran after him. Terrified, Larry ran as fast as he could along the railroad tracks across the street from our house. The boys caught up with him and tied him to the tracks with ropes. They ran away and Larry started screaming at the top of his lungs as he heard the train approaching. Praise be to God, a neighbor heard his cries for help and ran to him just as the train was approaching. He picked up an old glass bottle, broke it and used it to untie my brother. Larry related to me that he was too embarrassed to tell anyone about what happened that day.

Apparently, our father had taught him to "shadow box" to protect himself when he was very young. Larry tells me that our father said to him, "Hit first and ask questions later!" This advice came in very handy for my brother many times as he was growing up in Toronto during and after World War II.

There was a group of boys in the neighborhood who called themselves "The Gang of Seven." They were seven brothers and they delighted in hunting down Jews and beating them up. One day when Larry was about twelve years old, he and his friend Leo were strolling along in the ravine near Davenport Road. Leo was a Jewish war orphan who was being raised by an elderly Jewish woman. He was the only Holocaust survivor from his family from Europe. On this particular day, Larry and Leo's pleasant adventure turned into a battle for their lives. Suddenly, from behind them, they heard those familiar shouts, "Get those Jews!" The Gang of Seven came straight for Larry. Leo panicked, running as fast as he could down the hill, leaving Larry to fend for himself.

Apparently, Larry had gotten into a fight with one of the brothers the previous day and had pinned him down until he cried, "Uncle." Now, all seven were out for revenge for the humiliation suffered by their brother at the hands of a "Jew boy"! They formed a circle around Larry and decided to make it a "one on one" event. Out came the biggest fifteen year old boy Larry had ever set eyes on. He says that the kid looked like he had been body building since he was two years old! Larry said to himself, *Here's where I die!*

His survival adrenaline kicked in, and he tells me he just flew through the air and started sticking his fingers into his opponent's eyes and nose and mouth. The bully started screaming in agony. As the others came running to help, Larry took the opportunity to take flight, running away as fast as he could, eventually catching up to his friend Leo. Leo was trembling with fear so Larry walked him the rest of the way home. When the elderly lady who was caring for Leo came to the door and saw how dirty and disheveled the boys were, she smacked Leo across the head and chastised him for running around the streets like that. So, my brother never told anyone about this episode either.

There was another Jewish family on our street who later asked Larry to walk to school with their son Harvey, and act as his bodyguard. The word must have gotten around among the Jewish boys how brave Larry was, even though he didn't think of himself that way. He was simply fighting for his life. He told me that he never mentioned the scraps he had gotten into to anyone because he felt embarrassed and ashamed. It's amazing to me that I have never known these things about my oldest brother until now. I can see that God has had His divine hand of protection upon him from the beginning.

When Larry was fourteen years old, our father took him out of school. It was legal and not unusual in those days for a parent to do this. They had to go to the school and sign the child out if they were under the age of sixteen. Dad felt it was time for the oldest boy to go out and earn money to help support the family. That is the way our father had grown up and it was all he knew. He encouraged Larry to learn a trade as he had done when he was fourteen. At age fifteen, Larry was working at the Toronto Stock Exchange, which was also a common practice at that time. The boys were provided with uniforms to wear while working on the floor assembling the stock exchange numbers onto the boards and

Chapter 1

taking them down. One day while in the locker room, which had a marble floor, another employee started shouting and swearing at Larry because he was a Jew. Larry grabbed the guy's foot until the older boy fell with a heavy thud onto the cold, hard floor. He never bothered my brother again.

We all experienced anti-Semitism to some degree in our Gentile neighborhood. As kind and loving a person as our mother was, she was especially targeted for mocking and ridicule by some of our neighbors. After returning home on one of the occasions when she had been called a "Christ killer" and a "dirty Jew," my five foot mother stood cooking soup on our old gas stove.

As a six year old I loved to stand beside Mummy while she was cooking because, inevitably, she would let me have a little sample to taste. Just like the time that Gil and I exhausted Mummy when she was frying herself an onion sandwich on rye bread. As we stood there like two starving little urchins, Mummy asked us if we would like to try a little. She was sure that we would not like it but we kept asking for more! "If I keep giving you girls more fried onions, I won't have any left for myself!" This set us off to giggling as we gobbled up the rest of the onions, leaving none for our mother. Mummy laughed, "Oy vey! Next time I will eat MY sandwich first!"

On this particular day, the delicious aroma of homemade chicken soup drifted through the air and up my nostrils causing me to daydream of sitting down to eat those plump matzo balls and soft carrots that floated in a sumptuous broth that only my mother could cook. But I was jolted out of my daydream when my mother abruptly stated, "Rhonda, I don't know why they say we killed Jesus. He was one of us. Why would we kill one of our own?"

"Mummy, who's Jesus?" I asked.

"I think he was a doctor because I have heard that he healed a lot of people."

We never really talked of Him again, that I remember, but this short conversation awakened a yearning in my heart to know Him. For one thing, I wanted to ask Jesus why I was being blamed for His death and even more than that, why my gentle, kindhearted mother was being ridiculed because of Him. I kept these thoughts to myself as I continued to search for meaning in my young life.

I had some knowledge of God's existence and His involvement in my life from a very early age. Mother would never mention a person who had died without also saying, "God rest his/her soul." Also, I distinctly remember discussing God with some playmates at school when I was about seven or eight years old. We were looking up at the clouds in the sky and trying to figure out if God was a cloud since He was a spirit. One child said that God couldn't be a cloud because you can't see a spirit.

Jeremiah 31:33 and Hebrews 10:16 *But this is the covenant that I will make with the house of Israel after those days, says the LORD: I will put My law in their minds, and write it on their hearts; and I will be their God, and they shall be My people.*

Throughout my childhood, I had terrible nightmares from which I would wake up screaming until someone came to me. One night I awakened in terror from yet another nightmare. As my father and Kay, our nanny, came in and turned on the light, I was sure that I saw a demon from my dream slip down into a hole under my bed and disappear. Then the hole closed up. I tried to tell my father what I had seen, but he and Kay just kept telling me it was nothing but a bad dream. But I knew what I had seen because my eyes had been open. I knew I had not just been dreaming.

That glimpse into the spiritual realm of demons opened the door in my life to a fear of the dark. From that moment on until I was born again in 1982, I had to have a light on somewhere nearby when I went to sleep at night. I was afraid to even have one of my feet dangling over the edge of my bed.

Chapter 1

John 3:19-20 *"And this is the condemnation, that the light has come into the world, and men loved darkness rather than light, because their deeds were evil. For everyone practicing evil hates the light and does not come to the light, lest his deeds should be exposed."*

CHAPTER 2

"Oy Vey! The Children Don't Have Clothes For Such A Place!"

I remember my mother taking time to teach me the alphabet and how to tell time before I ever went to school. As the time approached for me to start kindergarten, my brother Stan painstakingly taught me to spell our surname, Middlestadt, along with teaching me to spell "Mississippi" forwards and backwards. One significant memory I have is of Stan walking me to kindergarten. It was a very chilly fall day and I was wearing a thin, navy blue cardigan and a short cotton skirt. I had my arms crossed in front of me to try to keep warm and Stan said, "Ronnie (as my siblings called me), put your arms by your sides and swing them. Hold your head up high and don't let Old Tom (the school crossing guard) know you are cold. If you keep moving your arms and legs like me, as if you are marching, you will soon be warm. Never, ever let anyone know how you are feeling!" I suspect that Stan may have used this tactic when he was made fun of for being a Jew. I recently asked him if he had experienced any anti-Semitism as had Larry. His answer was, "I managed to avoid it."

I have a faint memory of wearing special brown oxfords for awhile when I was very little. They were different than the shoes that the other children were wearing. I remember sitting on the cement stoop at the end of our front sidewalk, asking my mother, "Mummy, why do I have to wear these ugly shoes?"

She replied, "It's because you are special, Rhonda. And your shoes are not ugly, they are just different." This didn't satisfy me entirely, but if Mummy said it, it must be true, so I made up my mind not to think about it anymore.

As a young teenager I was always uncomfortable when I was sitting on the beach because my feet didn't seem to match up. I

Chapter 2

would squiggle around attempting to make them even but, no matter how I tried, there was always a bit of a difference in length. I used to hope that no one would notice. If they did, they never mentioned it to me, and I never brought up the subject. Gradually, through the years, I forgot about the length of my legs. Many years later, on the other side of the globe, I was to have an experience that would bring these memories back to me.

Mummy was an excellent and creative cook. Daddy often declared, "Your mother can make a banquet out of leftovers." However, baking was not her finest gift. Mother told me that just after she and my father had been married, she was so nervous about cooking for him that she baked an apple pie in the oven without making a crust for it. I asked her what Daddy did and she said that he just ate it as if nothing was wrong! As to her baking, I really enjoyed her hamentashen (a Jewish fruit filled pastry made during the Jewish holiday of Purim) and her raisin pie. Gilda always said that you could bounce Ma's hamentashen off the floor, but I really liked them, just as I preferred Ma's matzo balls which were hard and chewy as opposed to the soft, oily ones that our aunts cooked. Also, her chocolate cake was so moist, because it was not fully baked, but to this day that is the only way I enjoy a chocolate cake. It must be moist and gooey!

Our mother always wanted to make sure our father approved of her cooking. One of my most delightful memories is the family sitting down to eat dinner with Mummy leaning over towards Daddy to watch him take his first bite. "How is the food, Albert?" Once Daddy had tasted it and given his approval, we all could eat.

For a special treat, our mother's sisters, Bertha and Lil, would sometimes surprise us with bagels and pastries from the Jewish bakeries in their neighborhood. We were always delighted since there were no Jewish bakeries close to our home.

We also partook of baked delicacies from other cultures. Many a time when Gil and I arrived home for lunch from Huron Street school, there would be a treat of chocolate éclairs or a piece of German chocolate cake waiting for us that Mother purchased from the German bakery nearby on Dupont Street.

My father's name was Abraham Middlestadt. He was born on December 18, 1912. When he was a young boy in school he was bullied by the Gentiles as they teased him, calling him "Abie, the Jew". So, when he became a man, he changed his first name to Albert. From an early age, he was a gifted artist in sketching and painting. However, his talent was not appreciated by his family as they thought that he should "make something" of himself by taking up a trade.

He had once attempted to go to art school to develop his talent, but the instructor told him that there was nothing he could teach him. Instead he was asked to go around and help the other students to learn. He had a love for and a sensitivity to animals and nature that became evident in his artwork. Ma was so proud of Daddy's oil paintings. She had them hanging on all our walls. I also used to love them. Whoever visited our home would have to be shown his magnificent creations.

Our father told us one day that he ran away from home when he was fourteen years old. He had been abused by his stepmother who used to chase him with a butcher knife yelling, "I'm going to kill you!"

After he left home, Dad served as an apprentice in the printing industry. That was how he managed to have food and lodging while being out on his own at such a young age. The training he received enabled him to work later in life as a compositor at McLean's Magazine in Toronto before being employed as a lithographer at Rust Craft Greeting Cards.

Daddy left our house early each morning carrying a brown paper bag with a delicious lunch that Mummy had prepared. He boarded the streetcar to the greeting card factory or, on some occasions, was picked up from home by one of his buddies and rode to work in their car. He was nicknamed "Big Al" by the "boys" at the factory, although he was not even six feet tall.

Chapter 2

At night, after we had all gone to sleep, he would stay up and create water color sketches for a cartoon series that he named "Billy Beaver." They were very detailed drawings which he had dreamed of publishing as a comic strip. Unfortunately, no one seemed to be interested. I remember praying to God all through my childhood that my daddy would be successful. For extra cash, once a year during the Canadian National Exhibition, he would rent a booth and sketch caricatures for the public.

On occasional weekends, Daddy used to enjoy an outing at the old Woodbine race track to watch the harness races and sometimes try his hand at betting. He told us that when he was a youngster, he had a job walking the horses around the track. I remember one evening he bet on the winner and won a few dollars. So to celebrate, he purchased a giant pizza for the whole family. He came in the door beaming from ear to ear with that flat box sideways under his arm. We could smell the pizza from the other end of the hall and we all shouted, "Daddy, Daddy, don't carry it like that!" It was too late, of course. The pizza had already rolled itself to the end of the box.

Naturally, Mother sliced it anyway, just the way it was and quoted one of her favorite sayings, "It's not what the food looks like that matters. It's how it tastes." It tasted just fine. I think we ate the first original pizza rolls.

Our father was so enamored by Mummy's support that he tried out a new phrase he had just learned, "Thank you, Esther, my little cabbage."

"What did you call me? You called me a cabbage? Albert, I've never been so insulted!" Dad tried to explain that in French it was "mon petit chou" and meant "you are beautiful my cabbage," but mother would have none of it. I don't remember hearing that phrase again in our house.

Dad went fishing with his friends, Charlie and "the boys", on weekends during the summer. Charlie Heller owned the convenience store at the corner of Dupont St. and Davenport Rd.

where we would go for ice cream cones if we could get past Mrs. Heller's yipping Chihuahua. Then it was a challenge to get Mrs. Heller's attention away from reading the obituaries in the newspapers to attend to her customers.

One summer, Daddy had Gil and I toss a coin to see which one could go on a fishing trip with him. I won and all I remember is sleeping in the back of the car and being very bored as we sat in the boat on the lake for hours and hours. One time, my father took us girls and Mother fishing at Rice Lake and Mummy actually caught a bull frog on her hook. That was about enough fishing for Mummy, Gil, and me.

As youngsters, we would sit enthralled when my father took to story-telling, relating tidbits of his life during the Great Depression era. He told us that his father was a Jew from England and his Jewish mother was from Poland. When he was eight years old with three younger siblings, his mother died in the great flu epidemic of the 1920's. I remember seeing a snapshot of my father which he said was taken after his mother's funeral. There, on the pavement, stood a very sad looking little blue-eyed blonde boy dressed in a tweed jacket and britches. I don't think that sadness ever left his eyes. My grandfather remarried another Polish Jewish woman and had nine more children.

I only remember visiting Grandpa Middlestadt once when he was in the hospital. I remember thinking that he looked an awful lot like my father except he seemed to be really unhappy and gruff. He shouted at the nurses. My father said he was like that because he was sick and old. He lived in the east end of downtown Toronto on Boston Avenue which was where my father had grown up.

My father used to comment often that my brothers and sister and I were third generation Canadians. He said it was something to be proud of because not many people could say that. One thing he attempted to impart to us was a confidence that we could accomplish anything that we set our minds to do. One of his fa-

Chapter 2

vorite sayings was, "There are twenty-four hours in a day. That is more than enough time to do everything you need to do if you organize yourself." In spite of our annoyance at hearing Daddy utter this statement repeatedly, some of it must have rubbed off on my brothers. As two Jewish boys living in Toronto during that historical WWII era, they each successfully overcame their circumstances. Larry put himself through the Ontario College of Art and became a gifted and well-known fine artist. Stan attended the University of Toronto and became an electrical engineer. Stan had "skipped" two grades in elementary school which meant that he was only about sixteen years old in his first year at university. Besides having to survive being Jewish, he had the added difficulty of trying to fit in socially with much older students.

Larry was gifted with a strong baritone voice. When he visited, he would often practice singing his scales from the top front bedroom and Gil and I could hear him from all the way down the street on our way home from school. One year he sang and danced in the chorus line of "My Fur Lady", a musical satire first performed on stage in Canada in the 1950's. The music was a combination of 1940's tunes and 1950's rock and roll. There were also some jazz tunes, and the lyrics were a reflection of the political climate in Canada at that time. He toured with them for about six months.

One day, to everyone's surprise, Daddy proudly announced, "Esther, dress the children in some clean clothes. We are going to the theater tonight! Larry is going to be on stage at the Royal Alexandra!"

Mummy was thrilled. "Girls, Stanley, we are going to see your brother on the stage!" Suddenly she exclaimed, "Oy vey, Albert," as she clasped her hands to the sides of her face and looked up to the ceiling. "The children don't have clothes to wear to such a place like the Royal Alexandra Theater!"

"Esther, all that matters is that we are neat and clean. No one is going to notice how expensive our clothes are."

"Oy children, your father is right! Let's get dressed."

Gil and I giggled with excitement and anticipation as we washed and scrubbed ourselves for the big event. It wasn't everyday that we would be indulging in such an extravagant outing. In the early evening, we all piled into a Diamond Taxi Cab and off we went. Because of our big brother Larry, the Middlestadt family went to the theater! It was a most memorable experience for everyone.

I don't know when my father found his way to Detroit, Michigan where he lived for a few years during the Great Depression. Dad told us children that, while in Detroit, he often saw Al Capone's men driving around in cars with machine guns and that he witnessed gangsters pulling out huge rolls of cash from their pockets to entice naïve young men to join their organization. Of course, he was too wise to fall for their tricks.

My mother commented to me one day when I was a young girl, "Rhonda, when I first met your father, I was holding a broom in my hand!"

"Mummy, I exclaimed, that must have been so embarrassing!"

Apparently, Grandfather Wilson had a twin sister, Jennie, who met my father, Albert, while he was living in Detroit, Michigan. Aunt Jennie brought Albert to Toronto to meet my mother Esther, who was about twenty-five years old at the time. Albert was a few years younger. Imagine my mother's surprise when she realized that the handsome, well dressed young man that had come to visit her father that day had actually come to court her! Had she known in advance, she would have changed from her housedress and apron to more appropriate attire for the occasion. She would have unwound her braided hair to let her lovely, thick brunette curls fall softly onto her shoulders and back. Even so, her future husband found her to be very attractive.

After they were married, and my brother Larry was born, my father grew a moustache to make himself look older. He told me it

Chapter 2

was because he looked so young that everyone thought Larry was his little brother.

Because of the persecution my father experienced growing up, he refused to be identified as a "practicing Jew." This meant we did not celebrate the Jewish Sabbath or holidays at home or go to temple except to attend the weddings, funerals or bar mitzvahs of our relatives. Daddy, being a true "blue collar worker" hated wearing a tie for those special occasions and he would remove it as soon as possible afterwards.

Even though he refused to keep a kosher Jewish home, I find it interesting that he felt compelled to observe the holiest of the Jewish feasts with my mother. In the fall each year, she and my father always fasted on Yom Kippur (Day of Atonement), not even drinking water. When Mother was older, her doctor told her that for health reasons she could no longer keep the fast. This broke her heart as did the fact that my father would not allow her to have two sets of dishes or celebrate all the Jewish feasts like her sisters and brothers did. On Saturdays, because of her observant Jewish upbringing, Ma would always be saying things like, "Oh, we shouldn't be answering the phone," or "We shouldn't be writing on the Sabbath.

Our parents sometimes appeared to be playing a game with each other. No matter how many times this conversation came up, it would always be the same. It appeared to me like a rehearsed scene from a play. This is how it went. Mummy wants to tell Daddy something that she thinks might upset him. Mummy says, "Albert, promise you won't get mad if I tell you something."

Daddy replies, "Esther, just tell me."

"Not until you promise not to get angry," she insists. Daddy finally gives in and Mummy proceeds to tell him the bad news. As he begins to explode she calmly says, "You promised, remember?" I found this routine to be very amusing. They both spoke Yiddish fluently, so if they had something they felt little ears should not hear, they would converse in that strange language. Through the years, they spoke Yiddish less and less.

I used to love watching Mother as she embroidered pillow cases and table cloths for our home. I marveled at how she made it look so easy as she hummed a tune while she stitched the patterns with such dexterity. This was truly one of God's gifts to her. When I attempted to do it, I couldn't keep the threads from tangling on the wrong side of the material. My sister has a beautiful, intricate picture of an English cottage that our mother embroidered as a young woman.

> **CANADIAN JEWISH HISTORY**
> With the onset of the pogroms in Russia in the 1880's, rising anti-Semitism throughout Europe, the outbreak of World War I and Canada's post-confederation development efforts, many European Jews fled to Canada bringing the Jewish population of Canada to over 155,000 in 1930. Most of the immigrants who settled in Montreal or Toronto started out as peddlers but eventually established businesses, playing a leading role in the development of the textile industry. Following World War I, Canada changed its immigration policies, restricting the entrance of people who were not white Anglo-Saxon Protestant or from the United Kingdom. Following the Great Depression, even more immigration restrictions were imposed, derived, in part, from racial and religious prejudice. Despite attempts by the Canadian Jewish Congress, working alongside the social democratic party (the CCF), to enable the Jews of Europe to find sanctuary in Canada, Canada generally denied entrance to Jews, allowing fewer to enter than did other western countries. Of the tens of thousands of Jews seeking refuge during World War II, only 5,000 were allowed into Canada. Canada relaxed its immigration policy after the war, enabling some 40,000 Holocaust survivors to attempt to rebuild their lives there. www.myjewishlearning.com/history/Jewish_World_Today/Jews_Around_the_Globe/Canada.shtml "Canadian Jewry" by Sharonne Cohen

My maternal grandparents, Simon and Sophie Wilson, were among the Jews who fled Europe in the late nineteenth and early twentieth centuries. Mother often told me that my Zaide (Yiddish for Grandfather) Wilson came to Canada from Russia without a penny in his pocket and started out in business as a "Rags and Bones" man (another name for street peddler). She said he signed his name with an "X" because he had been a peasant living in a shtetl (Yiddish for small town or village) in Russia and had never learned to write. During a conversation with my Aunt Bertha this past year, she told me she remembered hearing that my grandfather's brother Frank, who had come to Canada ahead of Simon, had written to him to get out of Europe to escape the pogroms. Apparently, Simon and Sophie met and became engaged while making their way by train across Eastern Europe in order to emigrate to North America. They scavenged whatever scraps of food they were able to find and hid from attacking mobs in such places as haystacks on farmlands along the way. I assume they came to Canada by boat.

They settled in Orillia, Ontario and later moved to Toronto. Simon Wolnstein changed his name to Simon Wilson because, as my mother had related to me, he declared, "If the name Wilson is good enough for the President of the United States, it's good enough for me!" He was referring to President Woodrow Wilson who was in office from 1913-1921. Grandpa Wilson went from street peddling to establishing a thriving garment business in the west end of Toronto on Spadina Avenue. It was a women's clothing factory named Wilson Garments which specialized in coats and dresses and suits. After Zaide died, my uncles inherited the business and the name was changed to Wilbro (short for Wilson Brothers).

My mother used to take my sister and me to the Jewish Community Center on Spadina Avenue to look at Zaide's picture on the wall. I'm not sure if he was one of the founders or if he was one of the board members. As I recall, he had a chubby face inset with soft, gentle, laughing eyes that were decorated with a pair of simple, clear, round spectacles. His mouth and chin looked serious yet playful as he gazed out at me from the black and white photograph on the wall.

My Bubbie and Zaide Wilson experienced the tragedy of losing their first-born son. Harry was my mother's older brother and she told me that he died when she was twelve. Mother said she had really missed him as he had been the only one she could talk to who really understood her. He had apparently gone to a fortune teller and had been told that the next time he drove a car he would die. Harry became petrified of driving after that. Grandfather Wilson finally convinced him to take them (he, my mother, and Grandmother) for a drive in the family car. Sadly, they were involved in an accident and, while no one else was injured, Harry lost his life in the crash. Consequently, from hearing this story, I grew up with an unreasonable fear of driving. I had no problem riding as a passenger but I could not bring myself to learn to drive. It was to be much later in my life that I would conquer this fear.

Joshua 1:9 *Have I not commanded you? Be strong and of good courage; do not be afraid, nor be dismayed, for the Lord your God is with you wherever you go.*

II Timothy 1:7 *For God has not given us a spirit of fear, but of power and of love and of a sound mind.*

CHAPTER 3

"But, I Didn't Mean To!"

After the death of Grandpa Wilson, Mother often took Gilda and me to visit our Grandma Sophie Wilson (our "Bubbie"). We rode on the Avenue Road bus which let us off almost at the front door to Bubbie's house. Once inside, our favorite spot was the sitting room which always had an abundance of Licorice Allsorts set out in crystal glass dishes. Gil and I gobbled one after another of these yummy, sweet treats while doing our very best not to wipe our sticky fingers on the fine, flowered upholstery covering the hard-backed chairs we were sitting on. When Mummy finished talking with Bubbie in her bedroom, we were escorted in to see her for a short while before we returned home. As I recall, Bubbie was always on her bed watching her television when we visited. Her favorite program was Perry Mason and we often arrived during that time. I have no idea why she never, to my remembrance, left her bed while we were there.

Everything was very neat, orderly and clean which was in stark contrast to our house on Dupont Street. To me it was uninviting while our chaotic, messy home seemed adventurous and interesting. Even Grandmother's street, Oriel Parkway, felt like another world. To me, everything seemed so barren, not fun and adventurous like our street at home.

From my perception as a small child, Grandma Wilson never seemed to be too pleased with me. She usually commented about how untidy "Rhendela" (Yiddish for "little Rhonda") looked and never failed to mention to my mother, "Esther, can't you keep that child's hair out of her eyes. Here, put a bobby pin in it!" I really dreaded having to go into her bedroom and see her propped up against her two fluffed up pillows on top of her satin bedspread.

Chapter 3

She had curly, grayish hair and a round face with small age lines on her skin at the sides of her eyes. In my child's eye view, her legs, which were encased in heavy brown support stockings, stuck out of her dress like two little tree stumps. As Gil and I would approach she would exclaim, "Girls, girls, don't touch the bed. You'll make creases!" Then, she wanted us to put drops in her eyes and I would always push my little sister in front of me to make her do it. I never wanted to get too close to her. Her stern demeanor frightened me.

My mother's youngest sister, Aunt Bertha, lived upstairs from Bubbie with her husband, Uncle Will, and their two children, Sheri and Bobby. I remember Aunt Bertha and Uncle Will as being the only relatives that I felt somewhat comfortable with. Sometimes we were allowed to go and visit with them while our mother stayed with Bubbie or we were sent outside to play with our cousins. I couldn't help noticing the difference between myself and Cousin Sheri. Her nails were delicately manicured while mine were jagged and dirty. Her hair was shiny and neatly combed while mine was thick and unruly. Of course, Cousin Bobby complained about having to play with "the girls." Aunt Bertha's apartment, as my grandmother's, was clean and neat, but the atmosphere was different. I felt accepted there, and I sometimes had a fleeting desire to have the stability of an orderly home like Bobby and Sheri. Also, going upstairs meant I was able to get away from the critical gaze of my grandmother for awhile.

In the summer, Mother's two sisters, Aunt Bertha and Aunt Lil, occasionally took my sister and me to Bubbie's cottage at Lake Simcoe for a week. In contrast to when we visited Bubbie in the city, she was up and about at the cottage. She interacted with us much more at Lake Simcoe. I remember her telling us to be sure to only drink water that had been boiled and was stored in the refrigerator. We were not to drink water from the tap. Unfortunately, two incidents took place during those visits that were emotionally painful for me. Once, Gil and I were fighting over who was going to use the swing. We were each grasping and pulling opposite sides of the wooden seat when I decided to let my little sister have her way. I let go and screamed, "Okay, you can have it!" Of course, the corner of the swing seat flew at Gil and hit her on the side of her cheek just below her eye. Bubbie came running out of the cottage, cuddled Gil, and yelled at me for trying to kill my little sister! It was no use trying to explain that it was an accident. I longed for my Bubbie's approval, but it seemed to me that I could never be good enough for her.

Another episode was when Gil and I were getting out of our Aunt's car after arriving at the cottage. I got out first and hadn't noticed that my sister's hand was still holding onto the car door while I slammed it shut without looking behind me. Poor Gil was wailing as the door closed on her little finger. I quickly opened it and before I knew it Bubbie appeared seemingly from nowhere and shouted at me, "How could you do this to your little sister, you terrible mean little thing!"

"But Bubbie," I stammered, "I didn't mean to. I..." Before I could finish my tearful sentence, Bubbie and our Aunt had turned their backs on me as they rushed my sister to the house. It was a miracle that Gil didn't lose her finger! I do not think I was more than seven or eight years old at the time. As they ran to the cottage, I scurried off to my favorite place of solitude on the beach where I would watch the sun's rays sparkle and dance on the glistening water. The cool, refreshing summer breezes soon dried my tears as I became lost in my imagination where I would sail away on ships to faraway places full of adventure and intrigue.

I began to steal away to my secret place in the mornings before breakfast. There was one particularly smooth, round rock that I claimed as my own. I would climb up on it and there I would be on top of the world where anything was possible. I relished every moment until I would be jarred back to the present by the shrill voice of my grandmother calling me for breakfast.

Chapter 3

After her hospitalization, my mother often had seizures and fainting spells. As a young child, I was paralyzed with fear on those occasions. There is one time in particular that I remember. Gil and I were very young, perhaps around seven and eight years old. It was during the summer and, as usual, all our little friends were playing with us at our house. We ran into the house to find our mother lying on her back on the dining room floor, unconscious, drooling at the mouth, her body twitching uncontrollably.

The other children, perhaps about three or four of them, all gathered around her in curiosity. Gil and I ran to the front window to see if our father was coming home from work as it was about 5 p.m. in the afternoon. We sat transfixed on the sofa, not knowing what to do. As far as I remember, this was the first time that we had actually witnessed our mother having a grand mal seizure. Before that, we had seen her faint, but nothing like this. We felt totally helpless and afraid. The other children were asking us, "What is wrong with your mother? What should we do?" We just sat mute as we hoped our father would be home soon.

After what seemed like an eternity, Daddy walked in the front door and as soon as he saw Mummy, he shouted at all the children to get away from her and go home. "Oh, Esther, Esther, my darling Esther," he muttered as he knelt down to attend to her. After he helped her safely upstairs to the bedroom, he came into the living room to find us still sitting like little statues in fear. "How could you just sit there and do nothing while your mother was lying on the floor like that!" he yelled. "Your friends care more about your mother than you do!"

We just started to cry, "We're sorry Daddy; we didn't know what to do!" The whole event was very traumatic for the two of us. Even though my mother had suffered terribly, I do not remember her ever saying an unkind word to me about anyone. It was simply not in her nature to be bitter or self centered. If she was mocked or made fun of, mother would simply say, "Rhonda, I don't understand why people act like that." There was a man on our street who always walked with his shoulders slumped over and his head down. Mother would say, "Poor man, he must be carrying a very heavy burden to be walking like that on such a lovely, sunny day. How can he enjoy the beauty of the sky and the trees when all he can see is the dirty pavement under his feet? If he keeps walking like that he is going to bump into a lamp post and fall flat on his back. Then he will have to look up!"

She had a special ability to be able to make each one of us feel important. For example, at some point in our lives, my siblings and I all had thoughts that we might have been adopted. We never shared this with each other growing up. There was one really cute baby picture in our home that had been taken by a professional photographer and I remember asking, "Mummy, is that me?"

In her wisdom, she replied. "Of course dear, it is you." A few years ago I was together with my brother Stan and my sister Gilda and they both said that she had told them the same thing when they had asked! Now that we are grown, my sister and I can clearly see that the picture is of one of our brothers. Then again, it might be of one of our uncles! It remains a family mystery.

The equivalent in Canada of Girl Scouts of America is Brownies and Girl Guides. From age seven to eight, the group is called Brownies and they wear a brown uniform. From age nine to eleven, the group wears a blue uniform and is called Girl Guides.

When I was seven years old, I thought I would like to join the Brownies. I skipped along in eager anticipation with a few of the other children in the neighborhood to the Church of the Messiah at the end of our street to sign up. With excitement, we marched in and stood in a neat row in front of the administrator's desk. When it was my turn to be registered she smiled at me with her round cherub face and asked my name. "Rhonda Middlestadt," I announced boldly.

"Where do you live, my dear?"

Chapter 3

"I live at 73 Dupont Street." I was now feeling on top of the world. I had no idea what was coming next.

"What religion are you?" she asked politely.

I proudly answered, "I'm Jewish!" Suddenly, her smile changed to a stern frown as she slowly eased herself up from her chair, moving around to the front of the desk where she stood towering over me with her hands on her hips. I could now see her heavy set legs that were planted firmly over thick ankles encased in short white socks oozing out of her dark brown oxfords. In what seemed to me to be a loud, booming voice, she said "Why, don't you *know* that you can't come in here if you are Jewish! This is a *church*! You just run along home now." I, a seven-year-old little girl, stood in shock and humiliation in front of all the other children. As I came to my senses, I ran all the way home.

It was 1954 and Teresa, our cat, was pregnant again. We were all eagerly awaiting her new litter as the time grew near. The next thing we knew, Teresa was not pregnant anymore but her newborns were nowhere to be found. We searched all through the house and back yard but found no kittens. *What could have happened?* we wondered. October 15, 1954 was not only a memorable date for the city of Toronto when Hurricane Hazel struck with a vengeance; it was also the night that Teresa proved herself to be a heroic little mother. With the wind howling and torrents of rain pounding on the windows, Teresa stood meowing and meowing in the kitchen frantically scratching at the back door. We all suspected that the mystery of the missing kittens was about to be solved. My father and brother, Stan, armed themselves with flashlights, put on their rubber galoshes and raincoats, and headed out to follow this distraught little mother into the night. Mummy, Gil and I anxiously waited at home while Teresa led Daddy and Stan to her kittens where she had hidden them under a wooden fence in the back lane. It appeared to us that she had given birth there and didn't want to injure her babies by moving them too soon. She guarded them like a frenzied wild animal, not letting anyone touch them. So, our father and brother had no choice but to make several trips back and forth while Teresa carried each kitten one by one to the warmth and safety of our kitchen. Mother carefully and tenderly wrapped each frail, drenched little newborn in towels and blankets. After her ordeal Teresa was soon curled up with them, exhausted but content and purring through the night.

> Matthew 23:37-39 *"O Jerusalem, Jerusalem, the one who kills the prophets and stones those who are sent to her! How often I wanted to gather your children together, as a hen gathers her chicks under her wings, but you were not willing! See! Your house is left to you desolate; for I say to you; you shall see Me no more till you say, 'Blessed is He who comes in the name of the LORD!'"*

Sometime after the hurricane incident, my sister and I managed to convince our father to let us have a hamster for a pet. One night someone forgot to close the cage door after they fed the little creature and in the morning the cage was empty. It was winter and we had a coal furnace. The next day we could hear the little guy running through the pipes and we were terrified that he would end up in the fiery furnace. Well, our father painstakingly took apart the pipe on the basement ceiling which led to the furnace. We all watched and waited with baited breath as Daddy would exclaim, "Oh, he's getting closer" or "He's almost here." Daddy became a hero that day as he rescued Mr. Hamster just in time! Needless to say, we had no more hamsters after that.

I don't remember how Sandy, a part Spaniel puppy, came to be part of our family. He is the most memorable to me of the few pets we acquired through the years. Sandy used to hang around with Minerva, a Great Dane who lived at the end of our street. One day when my sister and I came home from school our mother had to give us the devastating news that Sandy had been run over by a car. He had been trailing closely behind Minerva as she ran across the street in front of an oncoming vehicle. The driver

Chapter 3

noticed the larger dog and slowed down to let her pass. But he did not see our short, tan colored pooch and, as he brought his car up to speed again, Sandy was hit head on. Our little hearts were crushed. At the dinner table that evening, we burst into tears and could not eat our food. I don't think Teresa minded, though, as she regained her position as the only pet in the family.

In our early years of growing up, our imaginations were encouraged and developed by the many radio programs available before television became popular. Gil and I used to hurry home from school to listen to each new episode of, "The Teddy Bears' Picnic." I have faint memories of our whole family sitting in front of our old RCA Victor radio listening to other shows such as "Amos and Andy". We also liked the scary radio show, "The Shadow". To enhance the event with the appropriate atmosphere, our big brother, Stan, would run around and turn out all the lights so we could listen to it in the dark. As I remember, this took place on Thursday evenings when our parents were out on their "bowling night." Mummy turned out to be an expert at the sport and almost always won a free turkey for Thanksgiving.

One day, a great surprise awaited us. Grandpa Wilson had purchased a television for our family. Up until that time, a little boy named Michael used to brag about the fact that he was the only kid on the street who had a television, and he wouldn't even let us in his house to take a look at it. This generous gift from our Zaide elevated Gil and me to celebrity status on the block as everyone promptly forgot about Michael. We invited all our little friends over to watch the test pattern, the Howdy Doody Show, Roy Rogers and Dale Evans, the Cisco Kid and the Little Rascals. Mom and Dad enjoyed the family shows with us such as, Our Miss Brooks, Leave it to Beaver, and Father Knows Best. One really old one was Ma and Pa Kettle.

It was a good thing that our brother Stan had a part time job at the hardware store. Whenever new tubes were needed for our television set, he was only too happy to oblige. He would dismantle it from the back to see what was needed, and then we would all hope that he would remember how to put everything back together again. Sometimes it took him a while as we surrounded him with anticipation. As long as Stan was able to re-assemble it before the Saturday night hockey game, he remained the child prodigy of the family. It is no wonder that he eventually became an electrical engineer.

Of course, the whole family gathered on Saturday nights during hockey season to watch Hockey Night in Canada. Often, our father gave my sister and me money to purchase hot mixed nuts from a shop called The Nut House, and we would all munch as we watched the game. Our mother had a knack of coming into the living room and standing directly in front of the television as she would ask, "Would anyone like a cup of tea?" completely oblivious to our frustration as we would hear the sportscaster's voice booming through the television behind her, "He shoots, he scores!"

Even Teresa, our cat, liked the television. Mother loved to feed the blue jays on our kitchen window sill. When Teresa would capture a bird in the yard, Mummy would promptly run out and free the bird while chastising Teresa. Every so often, Teresa would be very stealthy and slip past Mummy. Then we would find her sitting in front of the RCA Victor Television with her back straight, her exterior puffed up, her paws extended in front of her and her face peering at the screen as if to pretend that she was watching a show. Her ploy of innocence did not fool our mother as she stood towering over her with hands on her hips and remarked, "Teresa, what do you have there? I know you are sitting on something." Then, Mummy would grab the cat by the scruff of her neck and rescue the bird or in some cases a little mouse and put them back outside. This amusing routine was repeated on a regular basis.

While he continued to pursue a career as an actor, Larry succeeded in being cast in several television commercials. He was disappointed about having only "bit parts" as he called them, but

Chapter 3

we were all very proud of him. Our whole family would be filled with excitement as we gathered around the little black and white television to watch him. Daddy would jump up out of his chair and go right up to the screen while pointing his finger declaring, "There he is! There's your brother!"

"Where is he, Daddy, where?"

"Look, there he is, see the back of his head? I would know that head anywhere!" And that was Larry's moment of stardom. He didn't consider these television ads to be much of an accomplishment, but Daddy always reminded him of the residuals, saying that he would get paid forever for doing just one commercial!

Larry was also cast as one of the extras for the television series, "Last of the Mohicans" which was filmed in 1957 in what is now the town of Pickering, Ontario. He told us in animated detail of how he was lying on the ground in one scene when the actors who were playing the part of the settlers accidently rode over him with a covered wagon (they used real horses). To save his life he just kept rolling between the wheels. That is the story, according to Larry, of why he went bald as a young man.

He was also an excellent dancer and used to entertain everyone at Jewish weddings by performing Russian folk dancing. I remember the influence that Harry Belafonte had on him. He loved calypso and even bought the shirt to make his ensemble complete. My brother Stan had purchased a set of bongo drums after he saw Beaver Cleaver's brother, Wally, perform with them on the "Leave It To Beaver" show. That was all that Larry needed. He felt like a real calypso star as he played them. One day he let me try them. It just seemed to come naturally to me. That was when I first discovered my love for playing percussion instruments.

Psalms 150:4-6 *Praise Him with the timbrel and dance; Praise Him with stringed instruments and flutes! Praise Him with loud cymbals; Praise Him with clashing cymbals! Let everything that has breath praise the Lord. Praise the Lord!*

But I Didn't Mean To!

CHAPTER 4

"Go Fight Your Own Battles!"

Stan could not resist trying to scare my sister and me at night by howling into the radiator connecting his bedroom to ours. We just giggled and howled back through the radiator from our bedroom to his. We thought it was a lot of fun until Mummy shouted to us from downstairs to be quiet and go to sleep.

Stan and his friend Jimmy used to take Gil and me to the Canadian National Exhibition on "Children's Day" each year until we were old enough to go on our own with our friends. One summer, they took us to the Merry-Go-Round and told us to wait for them there when the ride was finished. They conveniently forgot to come back for us and, as we stood there crying, we were noticed by a policeman who took us to the "lost and found for children" until our brother came some hours later to claim us. We were probably about six and seven years old at the time. We really enjoyed being in the lost and found more than tagging along with Stan and his friend, especially the taffy apples and candy floss the policeman gave to us. I'm sure that God's angels were watching over us that day.

Stan redeemed himself the following winter when he took us to Ramsden Park to learn to ice skate. He and Jimmy went round and round the rink with us until we were confident enough to skate on our own. Once we had mastered the art of ice skating, Gil and I would often go to Ramsden Park to join the other children on the ice. We skated until we tired ourselves out, then walked home with our skates slung over our shoulders. As we plodded along, our frozen toes began to thaw while we envisioned the hot chocolate and marshmallows that would be awaiting us. On one occasion, we had piled into the park's wooden clubhouse at the

Chapter 4

top of the hill with our playmates to change back into our boots. After skating all afternoon, we were cold, hungry and ready to go home. Our friends challenged me to leave my skates on and glide down a steep icy path leading to the street. Since I was a bit of a daredevil, I was happy to oblige but half-way down the hill, I hit a bump and landed flat on my stomach! I couldn't even scream because the wind was knocked right out of me! Once again, God's angels were busy watching over me.

A pebbled back lane ran the length of our street for those who owned vehicles to drive through to enter their garages. It was a perfect play area for us as children. During summer vacations my sister and I would be up early and by about 7 a.m. we were already out in that back lane kicking up dust as we paraded along singing at the top of our lungs. Songs such as, "You Are My Sunshine," "I've Been Working on the Railroad," "Found a Peanut" and "Just Plant a Watermelon on My Grave" were some of our favorites, especially "You Are My Sunshine." I don't know how the neighbors put up with us.

One morning while my sister and I were out playing on the street, we saw a new family moving in at 57 Dupont Street. They were of Ukrainian heritage from the Canadian Prairies and had driven all the way from Kelvington, Saskatchewan in an old Ford car. We were on their doorstep early the next morning ringing the bell, or was it a brass knocker like ours? I honestly do not remember. Their mother answered and we asked if the girls could come out to play. "Why, it is so early. My girls are still sleeping."

"STILL SLEEPING?" we replied in unison. "Well, when they wake up, can they come out to play with us?" And so, began a foursome that continued into our high school years. Their names were Patricia (Pat) and Joanne (Joey). We were amazed when they told us that they wore snow shoes in Kelvington in the winter and that sometimes the snow was so deep they couldn't get out their front door! They had brought their snow shoes with them to Toronto and when we were older, the four of us used them to learn to play tennis before we were able to purchase real tennis racquets.

We had many adventures with our friends, Pat and Joanne, in our back lane. One moment the lane would be a baseball field. The next moment it was a scene from a cowboy movie. We were opera stars or hooligans; whatever our imaginations would invite us to be. When our mother would call us to come in for the night which always seemed to be earlier than the other children, our friends were on the lookout so Gil and I could run and hide. We would hear Ma calling, "Rhonda! Gilda!" until in frustration she would exclaim, "If you don't come here right now I am going to tell your father to come out!" That worked every time and we would appear from behind a fence or a tree or a garage.

Sometimes we were allowed to play in Pat and Joey's basement which we converted into a schoolroom. Pat always insisted on being the teacher because she was the eldest. We spent many enjoyable hours there acting out our school experiences and making up new ones.

If we went upstairs we would usually find their mother either looking through Sears catalogues to order clothes for her girls or baking cakes from boxed mixes, both of which we were not at all familiar with. One thing I do remember is that she prepared hundreds of potato perogies (boiled or baked dumplings of unleavened dough) every year and put them in the freezer. Their house would be filled with wonderful aromas when she was baking and cooking.

Their mom was a hairdresser and often had Pat and Joey's hair in pin curls while giving them a perm—a "Toni" as it was called then. At those times there would be a very strong odor of ammonia in their kitchen.

Their house always seemed to be so spic and span clean and very quiet compared to our home. What I remember most about their kitchen was the bright red linoleum floor that always looked as if it had just been polished. To us, it didn't even look as though anyone ate in there.

Chapter 4

In comparison, our kitchen was a small theater for my sister and me. We would sit at the old wooden table to watch Mummy clean a chicken that she had brought home from the butcher. We would wait in anticipation to hear her exclaim, "Oh girls, look, here's one chicky egg, no two, no three, no four!" It was such a thrill as our mother boiled those fresh eggs that she had just pulled out. It was a special treat just for us.

Also, when Daddy brought fish home from his escapades with Charlie and the boys, we would sit at that same table and watch Mummy scale the fish. The scales flew onto the walls, the floor, the sink; just everywhere!

Our mother never stopped us from running in the front door and out the back with our friends. She would just shout, "Girls, you look like you are going to a fire!" or "Girls, what do you think this is, a train station?"

When our little friends came to play, Mummy would always pinch their cheeks (especially Pat's as she was taller and thinner than the rest of us) and say, "Here, have something to eat. Tell your mother to let you stay with me for a few days, and I'll fatten you up and put some color in those cheeks of yours!"

Our mother did not use artificial or pre-mixed foods in her cooking. If she cooked a soup, she would start in the morning and it would simmer all day while a most irresistible, tantalizing aroma would fill the house. As an adult after I left home, I asked my mother how to make chicken soup or cabbage rolls. Her answer was always the same. "A little bit of this and a little bit of that." The one thing she told me about chicken soup was to put the meat in first; then, when the water begins to boil to be sure to take the scum off as it rises to the top before you add the vegetables or herbs and spices. "Then, you will have a sweeter and more pure tasting soup." This causes me to think of how when, as Believers in Jesus (Yeshua), we go through fiery trials, the impurities in our lives rise to the surface as we are being softened and molded into the image of our Lord. I never did ask Mummy how she made kugel or gefilte fish or chopped liver. Her kugel, which is a Jewish noodle dish, was out of this world as were her cheese blintzes, matzo balls, and borscht. I eventually learned to cook most of these dishes the same way, with a little of this and a little of that!

Often, Gil, Pat, Joey and I would play with our movie star cut-out dolls on our dining room table. We retrieved a tattered old cardboard box containing our treasured paper dolls from a drawer in the antique, dark walnut wardrobe in the corner of the room. Sometimes, we would be absorbed in our fantasy world of high fashion for hours and Mummy would have to remind our little friends to go home for supper.

We four girls were like the gang from the Little Rascals television series at times. Since we lived at Dupont and Davenport, Casa Loma was within walking distance for us to visit. We children did not visit the castle officially. We had no money for the entrance fee and, in any case, little ragamuffins like us were not allowed in without parental supervision. So, the four of us would hang around the entrance area until we noticed parents with children entering the castle. We strategized that we should only attach ourselves two to a family so as not to look suspicious. Then, we just boldly tagged along behind as if we were part of that family! Once we were inside, we had the most amazing adventures as we stealthily made our way through the many corridors and magnificent rooms of the castle. There was not the security system in place then as there is today or I am sure we would never have been able to pull off such a stunt. I do

> **CASA LOMA**
> There is a landmark in Toronto, a castle called Casa Loma, which was originally a residence for financier, Sir Henry Mill Pellatt. It was constructed over a three-year period from 1911–1914. Through a series of circumstances, the city of Toronto took over the castle in 1933. In 1937, this majestic structure was opened to the public as a tourist attraction. It is located at the north end of Spadina Road on an escarpment above Davenport Road.

Chapter 4

not believe we ever told our parents about our escapades on the Davenport escarpment.

Sometimes we played with a few of the neighborhood boys and one day they made fire arrows and were shooting them at us! We frantically ran as fast as we could down the street with the gang of little hoodlums behind us. We barged into the local hardware store where our brother Stan had his part-time job. We often went to Stan for his help when we needed it, and he always seemed to have just the right advice for us except for this time. From behind the counter, he shouted, "Go fight your own battles! Can't you see I'm at work?" Until that moment, we hadn't made the distinction between running to our big brother at home or in the store while he was working.

Our yard was what could graciously be termed as "a natural environment." The grass was left to grow wild while providing a home to bright yellow dandelions, tall stocks of wild rhubarb, and brightly colored hollyhocks. Our friends came to play there because we didn't have to worry about trampling on pretty little flower gardens. Our cat, Teresa, loved it, too. She would chew on the tall blades of grass as she crouched down, waiting to pounce on some unsuspecting bird.

One summer, our brothers built us a wooden fort in our backyard where we had many hours of fun with our friends. Pat, Joey, Gil and I decided to form a club, and that fort became our official clubhouse. We named ourselves the "Busy Beavers" in honor of our father's comic strip. We even made up a song with the words, "Busy Beavers are the busiest beavers in the world. They're always washing, scrubbing, cleaning. That's the way they work." We sang this song whenever we held our "meetings." We also sang our "Busy Beaver" song when we went door to door collecting old pop bottles to cash in for spending money. This, we did not do on our own street. I don't think our parents ever knew about our secret activities.

There are many ravines in Toronto and our mother would pack Gil and me a lunch to take as we started out early in the morning and walked from Dupont Street to the Don Valley which followed along the Don River. We managed to convince Pat and Joanne's mother to sometimes let them come with us. She admonished us to watch out for bears, which was something that had never occurred to us.

Today, the DVP (Don Valley Parkway) is a major expressway. It was a magnificent wooded area then with tall Maple, Oak, and Birch trees. We would wind our way along the path and cross over the streams on pebbles and finally end up at the old Riverdale Zoo. The old Zoo existed until 1978 when the new Toronto Zoo in Scarborough opened. The old zoo was in the heart of old Cabbagetown, originally consisting of the poor working class and lower middle class population. As the middle class began leaving, poorer people moved in and it soon became known as a slum. Today, the new Cabbagetown, which is north of the original, consists of restored Victorian homes and is a much desired neighborhood to live in. After we ate our packed lunches, we would wander around looking at all the animals. Later, we would take a little rest and then would walk, skip, and run all the way home.

Another pastime we loved was to sit on the stone slabs in front of the Church of Messiah, at the end of our street at Dupont and Avenue Road, on a Saturday when we thought there might be a wedding. We were rarely disappointed. We didn't mind the wait as we sat there like little street urchins watching for the bride to appear in all her radiant splendor. Wearing a long, flowing white gown, she appeared to glide or float along the pavement. To me, there was nothing more magnificent to be desired than to be that beautiful bride someday.

My father sometimes called me "princess" but, my mother used to laughingly say that when I was born she had told the nurses to take me away. She said that she thought I couldn't possibly be her baby because I had so much black hair that I looked

Chapter 4

like a little monkey. For years I imagined that I really did look like a monkey when I was born until one day when I asked my father about it. He told me that I had a lot of hair on my head but not all over my body. Unfortunately, the false negative image I had of myself was already set in my mind.

Pat and Joanne attended Brown Street School and also different high schools than us. Although we never went to school together we did see each other on weekends, holidays, and after school. Somehow, we remained friends all the way through our school years. My sister was close friends with Joanne well into their twenties, even renting an apartment together at one time. Pat moved out of the neighborhood, as did I, so she and I drifted apart.

Pat and Joanne's father was one of the neighbors that used to yell "Dirty Jew" and "Christ Killer" at my mother as she walked on our street. But it never stopped her from loving our two friends or from treating their mother with kindness and respect, especially when Pat and Joanne's father was dying of stomach cancer. Their mother eventually remarried and moved out of our neighborhood. But she had been a very positive influence in our lives until the end of high school.

Since our family did not observe Passover or any of the other Jewish feasts, I didn't understand why we were different when our Gentile neighbors were celebrating Easter. The ladies and gentlemen in our neighborhood flocked to the church at the end of our street wearing Easter bonnets, frilly dresses, smart suits and shiny shoes. I had no inkling of what it was about. All I knew was that it was a Christian holiday and we were not allowed to participate. I don't remember anyone ever telling me that it had anything to do with Jesus. It was a time for our friends to be hunting Easter eggs and eating candy. So that we would not feel left out, Gil and I conspired with each other about made-up candies we had received. When our friends gathered around to talk about all the goodies the Easter Bunny had brought them, we just chimed in about all of our delicious treats that we had enjoyed.

Christmas was a little easier because, for some reason, our parents felt that we could join in with the Gentiles a little on this happy occasion. Daddy used to send Gil and me to the Cigar Store on the corner to pick out a small Christmas tree which we would drag home. Our family called it a Hanukkah Bush! We even had a glittery red star to put on top. Also, Gil and I were allowed to purchase coloring books for each other as gifts to put under the tree. When we were very little, we were sent to bed early to wait for Santa Claus to arrive. We even wrote letters to Santa one year and one Christmas Eve, Gil and I sneaked down to the second floor hallway after we had been sent to bed to hear our parents wrapping a few gifts for us. There was one very special Christmas when our big brother Larry surprised us and came to visit bringing all kinds of presents for everyone. I still remember the bright red, toy carpet sweeper that he gave me. Gil and I got more than coloring books that year!

John 10:22-25 *Now it was the Feast of Dedication [Hanukkah] in Jerusalem, and it was winter, And Jesus walked in the temple, in Solomon's porch. Then the Jews surrounded Him and said to Him, "How long do You keep us in doubt? If You are the Christ, tell us plainly." Jesus answered them, "I told you, and you do not believe. The works that I do in My Father's name, they bear witness of Me."*

Growing Up

CHAPTER 5

"Maybe Next Year"

During my early childhood years, my mother imparted to me a love for reading and writing. She took me to the library often and read to us from Aesop's Fables. She also recited many nursery rhymes from memory, such as, "Hickory Dickory Dock" as well as long poems, such as, "The Spider And The Fly." After I learned to read, I enjoyed "The Bobbsey Twins" and "Raggedy Ann" comic books. As I matured, two of my favorite authors were Charles Dickens and Louisa May Alcott. I enjoyed Louisa May Alcott's book, *Little Men* more than *Little Women* as I was somewhat of a tomboy. When I was about eleven years old, my imagination was captured by the Dickens novel, *The Old Curiosity Shop,* which was first printed as a book in 1841. I noticed it in Stan's bedroom on one of the mornings that I had to wake him up for school. It was a small, thick, maroon colored, leather bound book. Stan noticed me lovingly holding it. "Would you like to read that book, Ronnie? You might be a little too young for it though."

"Oh Stanley, could I, could I, please?"

"Sure," he replied. "Just take good care of it, okay?" I cherished that book as I stepped into its pages. Little Nell and her grandfather became so real to me in their plight and my heart broke when Nell died.

I longed to write like that. I wanted to write about things that really mattered and to be able to do it in such a way as to bring the reader into my story as if they were living it. I mentioned to my father that I would like to be a writer someday and that my teachers all said I had a talent for it. "That's a wonderful ambition Rhonda," he told me.

"But Daddy, how do I do it?" I asked.

"Well, if you want to be a writer, you just need to write."

Chapter 5

"But what do I write?"

"Rhonda, just start by writing down things that happen in your life. Before you know it, you will think of lots of things to write about." That was an excellent piece of advice from my father that, unfortunately, I did not take.

As an adult, I have been inspired by biographies and autobiographies of women who have made a difference in the world. One of my favorite women is Golda Meir, born Golda Mabovich, May 3, 1898 in Kiev, Russian Empire, which is present day Ukraine. Who would have thought that this little girl who emigrated to the United States with her family in 1906 would become the fourth Prime Minister of the State of Israel in 1969?

I had one friend who loved reading as much as I did. Her name was Genevieve. She was a real book worm and we used to enjoy going to the library together. One day, she asked me to stay overnight at her house. I was still in elementary school, perhaps around grade four and my parents were reluctant to let me stay the night but after much pleading on my part they finally agreed.

Just as we were bedding down, Genevieve asked if I could keep a secret. Of course, I replied enthusiastically, "Yes."

Then she told me, "The bed you are sleeping in tonight is my little brother's, and he has been really sick with scarlet fever, and my mother has not had time to change the sheets. Please don't tell anyone because my mother could get into a lot of trouble. You have to promise that you will not tell a soul." Of course, I had no idea how serious this was so I promised her and we drifted off to sleep. I remember waking up the next morning with a throbbing headache and feeling weak and sick to my stomach. I left without having breakfast and walked home as quickly as I was able. By the time I arrived home I could barely stand up. As soon as I came in the door my parents could see that something was terribly wrong with me. They laid me on the sofa in the living room, took my temperature and called good old Dr. Giddens to tell him I had a raging fever and to please come immediately to the house.

After the doctor examined me, he asked me if anyone in my friend's family had been sick but I was certainly not about to break my promise to Genevieve so I said, "No." To tell you the truth, I imagine the doctor and my parents did some investigation of their own and all I know is that I was never allowed a sleepover again.

Carla, a cute, short lady who rented the rooms on the second floor of our house for a time, helped to take care of me while I was sick with scarlet fever. Our house was quarantined and I was prescribed penicillin in what seemed to me to be the most gigantic, round, pink pills I had ever tried to swallow. Carla used to come in the middle of the night to awaken me to take one. I was laid up for a few weeks, as I recall. When I was finally able to go outside again, Carla decided to take my sister and me for a ride in the country in her car as she said the fresh air would be very good for me. Our aunts were the only women we knew who had their own vehicles, so this was a rare occasion for us indeed.

I felt wobbly and weak for awhile but it wasn't long before I was back to my old self, running and playing softball with the other children. There was no more special treatment for me and before I knew it, I was back to day dreaming and getting myself into trouble.

I will never forget my fourth grade teacher, Ms. Black. I had been put into the advanced stream to do second, third, and fourth grades in two years, so I was young for a fourth grader as were the others in my class. I was so happy to be back at school after being sick with Scarlet Fever for, what seemed to me, to be an eternity. As was her practice, Ms. Black began our morning by reading a Bible verse. I must have wandered off in my mind to some imaginary place because I was suddenly startled to hear our teacher shouting, "Rhonda Middlestadt, this is the third time I have told you this morning to throw out your gum!" I made it worse by telling her that I had not heard her. I was ordered to spend recess in the cloakroom with my face towards the wall. This was such a humiliation because the children all made fun of me as they

Chapter 5

passed by on their way to the school yard. But what caused me the most pain was the fact that I was telling Ms. Black the truth. I really didn't hear her. I must have been day dreaming.

Another frustrating time when no one believed me was when I accidentally opened the bathroom door at home on Mr. Hubble, one of our boarders and saw him on the toilet. I was only about eight years old and I just stood there in shock with my mouth open while he yelled at me to close the door. He thought I had opened the door on purpose as a prank. When I came to my senses, I ran down the hallway and threw myself sobbing across my parent's bed. I cried over and over, "I didn't do it on purpose," while Mummy gave me a lecture about little white lies becoming big black ones.

When I was about twelve years old, I had a silly crush on our paperboy who lived on the other side of the street. One summer evening, as I sat on our front steps with the garden hose in my hand watering the front lawn, he came towards our house carrying newspapers under his arm to make his delivery. I was staring at him, wondering what I could say, when all of a sudden he was soaking wet, papers and all, and screaming at me. My father came charging out the front door behind me about the same time as the boy's father came running across the road to our house. I was amazed to find out that I was to blame! My hand that had been holding the hose followed my eyes towards him. I was really in trouble for day dreaming that time! Daddy sent me to my room as he battled it out with the paper boy's father. Once again no one would believe me when I said I had not done it on purpose. Such was my life.

Besides the paperboy, we had a bread man, a milkman, and an egg man. Our milkman used to make deliveries with a horse drawn truck. As Gil and I heard the clip clop of hooves, we would gleefully run to our mother who handed us sugar cubes to give to the horses.

On Friday evenings during dinner our delivery men would come to the door one by one to collect for the week, the paper boy usually arriving first. It was always as if our parents never knew they were coming. The rhetoric would go something like this; "Who could that be at such a time as this Albert?" or "Esther, didn't we just pay the bread man?"

"Albert, that was last week already." And so it would go until they had all been paid.

Even though Grandfather Wilson had purchased the house on Dupont Street for our parents, our father had many medical expenses because of the medications needed for our mother. We didn't have any such thing as a Universal Health Plan or, for that matter, any kind of a health plan in those days. Daddy would always proudly say, "We may not have much money but my children always have plenty of food to eat and clothes on their backs."

A time that I wished our family had more money was when I was in grade five. I had been invited to a birthday party by the richest girl in our school. In the winter, Maybeth wore a one piece green snow suit, a luxury in those days, with white fur around the hood. The rest of us were a little envious of this pretty little blonde girl. We dressed with separate leggings and jackets because our skirts had to be showing outside of our snow pants. Girls were not allowed to wear slacks to school. Maybeth was able to bypass that ruling since it would be impossible for her to do so in a one piece snowsuit.

I had no idea how I was singled out to go to her party. I wasn't particularly enthusiastic about it because I imagined she lived in some kind of a mansion and what would I wear to a rich girl's party? Worse still, I had no way of purchasing a gift for her! My mother came up with the brilliant idea that I could give her my little red patent leather purse. "But, Mummy, she will know it's not new!"

My mother replied, "Look Rhonda, we'll shine it up and wrap it in pretty paper and Maybeth will never know the difference."

Chapter 5

I had terrible visions of arriving at the party and everyone pointing to me saying, "Look, Rhonda couldn't even bring a new gift." The day arrived and I hesitantly climbed the stone steps up to Maybeth's front door, gingerly ringing the bell. I shyly produced my gift and, to my utter amazement, my mother was right. She loved her little red purse, and I was relieved and enjoyed myself. I even forgot how much I loved that purse myself.

Not long after that birthday party, the school dentist checked all the students' teeth and sent a note home to my parents that one of my teeth had a cavity. My mother set up an appointment for me with Dr. Hord and the dreaded day arrived. The cracks in the sidewalk seemed to rush under my feet in a never ending rhythm as I tried to slow my pace in an attempt to avoid the inevitable. "Rhonda, we're going to be late for your dentist appointment," Mummy said as she took my hand firmly and prodded me along. "I know you are afraid but just think of it this way. Tomorrow, you will be walking along this same street to school and the dentist appointment will have been yesterday!" It didn't help me to forget about what was ahead of me that afternoon, but this was not the first time my mother imparted a spirit of hope to me that would prove to be invaluable during many trying circumstances later in my life. No matter how dark the night may be, the morning will always come and there will be the dawn of a new day. What a miracle that is.

Psalm 30:5 *Weeping may endure for a night, but joy comes in the morning.*

My father also unknowingly kept that spark of hope alive in me. When I was in elementary school, I read the book, *Black Beauty*, by Anna Sewell. I was captured by the enduring tale of this beautiful black horse. After I read that book, every year on my birthday I would ask my father if this would be the year that he would buy a ranch and some horses, to which he always replied,

"Maybe next year." That gave me hope until I was old enough to understand the realities of life and finances, but I am thankful for those years that I was able to dream.

Later, as a young teenager, my sister told me that her Scottish girlfriend Cathleen had a cousin who lived on a horse ranch just outside of Toronto. I begged my parents until they let me go to that ranch upon occasion to learn to ride. I was thrilled when Davey would arrive in his dirty old pick-up truck to transport me there. I thoroughly loved every minute of it, even walking the horses around the corral after a run to cool them down. I especially enjoyed the speed of galloping with the wind whooshing through my hair. I felt so free during those precious moments. To me, horses were magnificently beautiful creatures. I was in awe of how sensitive they were to me and how aware they were of my every move. I had not known such oneness with an animal before. I had a desire to fly through the air on my trusty steed while leaving the cares of my earthly existence behind.

Revelation 19:11-16 *Now I saw heaven opened, and behold, a white horse. And He who sat on him was called Faithful and True, and in righteousness He judges and makes war. His eyes were like a flame of fire, and on His head were many crowns. He had a name written that no one knew except Himself. He was clothed with a robe dipped in blood, and His name is called The Word of God. And the armies in heaven, clothed in fine linen, white and clean, followed Him on white horses. Now out of His mouth goes a sharp sword, that with it He should strike the nations. And He Himself will rule them with a rod of iron. He Himself treads the winepress of the fierceness and wrath of Almighty God. And He has on His robe and on His thigh a name written: King of Kings and Lord of Lords.*

CHAPTER 6

"Where Do I Belong?"

Brrrr! I pulled the woolen cap tightly over my ears, snuggling my chin and mouth into the soft cuddly scarf tied loosely around my neck. There was a bitter chill in the air. I hugged my sixth grade books tightly to my chest, opening and closing my fingers inside my mittens to keep them warm, as I hurried home from school ahead of my little sister and her friends. Oh, how glad I was to scurry up our front steps, fling open the door, and release my burden with a loud thud to the floor. The loving warmth inside was in sharp contrast to the arctic cold outside. My toes began to tingle as they started to thaw.

"What's to eat, Ma?" I shouted as I tossed my jacket over one of the many hooks in the hallway. There never seemed to be enough for everyone. Our coats and sweaters were always doubled up to share space. The kitchen was my favorite room after school and I ran there to greet my mom who glanced up quickly to "Shhshh" me as she ladled some hot steaming soup into a bowl, saying to the man she was serving, "Eat, eat, it's good for you!"

I saw him from the back, hunched over the wooden table, a burly, unkempt form with scruffy, curly hair, and scraggly pants. As I moved around the table, I saw that he had a bushy bearded face. He slurped the delicious homemade soup gratefully. For the moment, I forgot about my own hunger as I watched him eat. Mother gave him huge chunks of fresh bread to dunk in his soup, but I noticed that he stuffed them into his pockets instead. I wondered where or when he might be eating his bread. I thought perhaps it might be as he bedded down for the night in some shelter, or even in an alley, to stave off the hunger pangs for the night.

Chapter 6

Soon, he was finished and as Ma ushered him out of the house with a full, warm stomach, Daddy arrived home from work. When the man was safely out of hearing range, Father said again those famous words that I had heard so often. "Esther, Esther how many times have I asked you not to bring strangers in the house when I am not here?"

Mother replied as always, "But Albert, Albert, he was hungry and cold. How could I turn him away?"

Albert knew his Esther. He knew that she was not going to stop feeding the hungry when they came to her door, but he felt it was his duty to speak up to protect his family. If the truth were to be known, he adored this quality in our mother, as did we.

And so it was that often, on a cold winter's day I would arrive home from school to find my mother warming the stomach and the heart of a stranger.

Proverbs 19:17 *He who has pity on the poor lends to the LORD, And He will pay back what he has given.*

Hebrews 13:2 *Do not forget to entertain strangers, for by so doing some have unwittingly entertained angels.*

Now, the "Fuller Brush Man" was another story. He was a salesman going door to door to sell household items and Ma had a knack of obtaining every sample that he had available before sending him on his way. I don't remember her ever purchasing anything although she may have. It was a mystery to me how he was so persistent in returning to our house only to go through the whole routine again. Perhaps he enjoyed lightening his load so he didn't have so many samples to carry on the rest of his route.

Our mother was a very simple woman. There was nothing pretentious about her. She and her friends used to greet each other as Mrs. or Miss so and so. One neighbor and friend Mrs. A. came over on a regular basis and as it turned out, she was a kleptomaniac. Ma would have her in for tea and she would always ask if she could go down to the basement to collect a couple of old newspapers before she went home. Of course, she didn't just take newspapers. She would gather up anything that was available before leaving. Ma knew what she was doing but didn't have the heart to confront her. She would say, "Poor Mrs. A, her husband is so strict and stingy with her. She has to account for every penny she spends at the grocery store. She probably needs the things that she takes."

Daddy would come home from the factory and ask, "Did Mrs. A go down to the basement before she left today?"

Ma would answer, "Albert, you know I always give her the old newspapers to read."

Daddy would then go to check if anything was missing and sure enough, something always was. Then the famous words would come forth from my father's lips "Esther, Esther, how many times have I asked you not to have that woman in this house?"

"Yes, yes, I know, Albert. I'll make sure she doesn't go down to the basement by herself next time." And so it would continue.

There were other times that our parents were quite a comical pair. If Daddy was reading the newspaper, inevitably, as he began to turn the page Mummy would say, "Wait, Albert, I'm not finished with this side yet."

He would reply, "Esther, Esther, how many times have I asked you not to read the other side of the paper while I am reading it."

It was Friday night and at the age of 11, I was already going out on my first "date". I waited anxiously for Harvey to arrive to walk with me to Huron Street School's movie night. The students would sit on the floor and watch the film that was run from an old projector onto a large white screen in the kindergarten room. For some reason, the only movie I ever remember seeing there was Swiss Family Robinson. I'm not sure they had any other movies. There were also a variety of games to play in the gym.

I had met Harvey while rehearsing with an amateur theater group called West End Players. I believe I was in grade six or sev-

Chapter 6

en when my brother Larry came home one day and told Gil and me that there was an opportunity to audition for a part in a play. They were looking for a girl to be cast as a boy in a family drama. Larry was a member of the group and told them he had two sisters who could audition. I got the part and so began my very short career as an actress. We performed in school auditoriums, and I really enjoyed it until the night that my parents came to see me. I noticed them from backstage and I froze in sheer terror. I went totally blank and the adult actors told me to keep taking deep breaths. They brought out my understudy just in case, but I managed to get through it. I was so afraid of making a mistake in front of my family. I had always felt that I was never perfect enough.

Harvey was the son of the actor who played my father and he used to come and watch us rehearse. I developed a terrible crush on him and begged my mother to let me have a pair of white stockings instead of the heavy brown ribbed ones I wore. She would not hear of it and I felt like such a peasant, thinking that Harvey would never notice me.

One day to my astonishment, I got up the courage to ask him if he would like to go to the Friday night movies with me. To my amazement, he said yes! My parents gave me permission to go with Harvey and when Friday night rolled around, he showed up at the door with his father! His father said he had no problem with us going to the movies as long as he could come too. So, that was my big date with Harvey and, to be honest, I was really glad that we were not allowed to go alone. I suspect that my parents and brothers had a hand in this arrangement.

One group of actors at West End Players was rehearsing a play about Noah's Ark, and I used to take the streetcar early to my rehearsals so I could watch them. I was very curious about the story but had no idea how to find out more about it. I knew nothing about the Bible and had no idea who Noah was. This knowledge was to come to me much later in my life.

It was September, 1956. The crisp early morning air burned in my nostrils while my chest ached and my legs felt like rubber. Still, I pressed on. With my face set to the wind, I pushed my body to the limit and crossed the finish line inches behind my arch rival, Diana. Second again! Every year since third grade I had competed in the 100 yard dash track and field event. Diana with her long braids gathered on top of her head would always finish the race just seconds ahead of me.

Any sprinter or long distance runner knows that when you are in a race, you must not look to the left or to the right to see what the other runners are doing. It will slow you down and may even trip you up. I tried my best not to be distracted by Diana but I was not always successful.

My one goal in seventh grade was to be the winner. Oh how I wished that Diana would forget to tie her hair up. I was sure that her thick, heavy hair would slow her down just enough to give me time to get ahead. Those few seconds of day dreaming about her hair falling down while we were running may have cost me the race more than once. Nevertheless, I continued with perseverance to compete while I would imagine myself winning with the crowds cheering me on.

I was about to realize my dream but not exactly in the way that I had envisioned it. Diana and I were members of the relay team for our school that year. The coach placed me as the last runner and Diana as the second to the last runner. We were falling behind. As I stood positioned to take the baton with my outstretched arm behind me, my body bent forward, and my head turned slightly to watch for the runner, I could see Diana leaving a cloud of dust behind her as she burst ahead of the other competitors. As she drew close, my heart pounded with excitement. I could hardly stand still as I waited for the baton to be passed to me. The moment came and in a flash I was off and running. There was no time for fear. There was no time to contemplate whether I could keep the lead. This was what I had been trained for! This

Chapter 6

was my moment! I ran as I had never run before. The crowds were cheering "Rhonda" "Rhonda" "Rhonda." I could hardly feel the ground beneath my feet. I could hardly feel my feet at all! It was as though I was flying. I crossed the finish line first and a triumphant roar went up from our school team.

If it wasn't for Diana bringing us up front, I don't know if I ever would have experienced my glorious moment of victory. Instead of envying Diana, I now appreciated her and understood the importance of helping each other to achieve our dreams. Later that year I injured my knee in an ice skating accident which prevented me from competing in eighth grade, my final year in elementary school. I was disappointed that I couldn't run but so glad that I had the opportunity at least once to experience the thrill of being first to cross the finish line.

> Hebrews 12:1-2 *Therefore, we also, since we are surrounded by so great a cloud of witnesses, let us lay aside every weight, and the sin which so easily ensnares us, and let us run with endurance the race that is set before us, looking unto Jesus, the author and finisher of our faith, who for the joy that was set before Him endured the cross, despising the shame, and has sat down at the right hand of the throne of God.*

After fulfilling my dream of being the first runner to cross the finish line, I was encouraged in my heart to cross yet another hurdle. I was old enough now to join Girl Guides and with new-found confidence, I set out to do just that. I marched down the street to the Church of the Messiah to register. Miss McBride was the new administrator and I found her to be a jolly, fun spirited person. It didn't seem to matter to her at all that I was Jewish. On the contrary, she welcomed me into the fold. I was given a blue uniform with red tie and blue beret and, for a while, I really felt that I belonged. I excelled at floor hockey and, much to my surprise, was made the captain of my team. I had no idea how I could have been chosen because I surely did not aspire to be a leader; it just seemed to happen to me at school and now at Girl

Guides. I even spent one winter weekend at camp in the country, eating oatmeal porridge that we cooked in a huge iron pot and learning survival techniques in the snow. I also attended Girl Guide summer camp that year and the only lonesome time was on Sunday morning because the whole troupe went to church without me. Because I was Jewish, I was told I had to stay in the camp alone until they returned. I remember thinking that I really would have liked to go with them but I was too shy to make a point of it.

I do not remember our friends, Pat and Joanne joining Girl Guides. My sister has recently told me that she was a member of the Girl Guides for the shortest time on record – one day! In any case, I used to go across the street to collect our friend Crystal who would walk to the meetings with me. Crystal and her family were the only Germans on our section of Dupont Street. Crystal and her brother, Norbert, told us that their father and mother had escaped Germany during the war in a small boat. As I remember, their house was immaculately clean and had a strong lemony scent of floor polish. Mrs. J was, to our knowledge, the only mother on our street who worked at a job outside of the home. When I arrived at her door, Mrs. J would ask me in so that she could straighten my tie and hat but I never felt as neat and tidy as Crystal in her starched and pressed uniform.

From a very young age, I felt like I was walking in a vacuum at school. I knew that I *"was"* Jewish but did not know anything about *"being"* Jewish. I knew I wasn't a Gentile but I didn't know what that meant either. So, I avoided school as much as possible by playing hooky whenever I could. While I was in seventh grade at Huron Street School I feigned a sore knee one morning. My mother even had Dr. Giddens come to the house to have a look at me. Of course, he could find nothing wrong. When my little sister came home for lunch, she told me that Mr. Everett, my teacher, was having a party in the afternoon. I had a sudden

Chapter 6

recovery and enthusiastically went to school. As I sat at my desk, anticipating the festivities, my teacher took the note I had handed him and said out loud for all to hear, "Sore knee, eh?" as he looked me straight in the eye. Oh, the shame and humiliation of it all! At recess, some of the Jewish children told me that they had told Gil to tell me there was a party so I would come to school for the history test. Apparently, it was obvious to all that I was the great pretender!

I had not studied for this test and there soon developed a tug-of-war between my Jewish friends who wanted me to study and my Gentile friends who wanted me to skip rope. They almost ripped my arms from their sockets as one group pulled me from side to side screaming, "she's coming with us to study" while the other group pulled me to their side shouting "she's coming with us to play skipping" until I finally cried, "Stop! I will study for the test!"

Life continued as usual until one night when I awoke suddenly from a deep sleep. It was still dark and I did not recall hearing a noise. I rolled off of my side of the bed so as not to awaken my little sister and as I stood to my feet a sudden wave of nausea swept over me. I staggered to the staircase and held on to the banister tightly while it seemed to take an eternity to get down to the second floor to my parents' bedroom. By the time I opened their door my head was reeling as I managed to make it to the side of their bed and call out before I fainted in a heap across them.

The next thing I remember was my father running through the house opening all the windows and my mother waking up the family. It was in the middle of winter and bitterly cold. We were all throwing up while Mother went from one to another to clean up our mess. It is still a wonderment to me how she was able to do it as she surely must have been feeling ill herself. Dr. Giddens was called and arrived with his little black bag to check everyone over. He said it was a miracle that I had woken up because the house was full of carbon monoxide fumes and we all would have died in our sleep. It turned out that our neighbors had erected a new television antenna on their roof and some of the debris from their side landed on top of our chimney. God was surely watching over us that night!

Another experience of God's miraculous protection was when my sister and I, along with our two friends, Pat and Joey went on a ride called the "Scrambler" at the Canadian National Exhibition during summer vacation one year. It was one of our favorite rides. Four to a car was allowed, so we ran up the wooden ramp with our tickets and piled into one car together. This one particular time, I was the last one in, so it was up to me to close and latch the safety bar. I noticed that the ride was starting and I hadn't been able to lock us in yet. I was in a panic as I shouted to the operator to tell him we were not ready. Even Gil and our friends were oblivious to what was happening. As the cars started moving faster and faster, I clutched the bar as tightly as I could with both hands while leaning against the side of our car for support. Everyone was screaming hysterically as we jolted forwards and backwards and side to side spinning around. God must have sent an angel to hold that bar in place to keep us from falling out. I surely know that I was not strong enough to do it myself. I was so glad to walk down the ramp on my wobbly legs after everything had come to a standstill.

At the start of eighth grade, I was transferred, along with my sister who was in seventh grade, to Jesse Ketchum School on Davenport Road. This was the beginning of what they called "Junior High School". It consisted of grades seven and eight, which was to prepare the students for high school by having a schedule allowing us to move about to different classrooms and teachers for various subjects in the curriculum.

As I sat on the bench outside the principal's office I tried to figure out what kind of trouble I had gotten myself into. I decided that my art teacher must have reported me as she was always

Chapter 6

threatening to send me to the principal for talking too much in class. I waited in the shadowy hallway, perched on the edge of the slippery, shiny wooden bench. Finally, the secretary stuck her head out the door. I slid off the bench and timidly made my way into the office. I trembled as the principal towered over me, but was surprised to find that I was not there to be reprimanded after all. He had summoned me because a new student named Judy was coming to the school, and he felt that she would need a friend.

Judy was a European immigrant who wore very thick, ugly eye glasses. I thought to myself, "*Why me? I'm timid and I like to keep a low profile at school. I don't want to be noticed and if I have to hang around with Judy, I'm going to stand out like a sore thumb!*" To top it off, I found out that she was Jewish. "*That does it,*" I thought, "*I'm finished! Now everyone is sure to find out that I'm Jewish too! This is Jesse Ketchum School. It is not a safe place like Huron Street School. We were mostly Jewish kids there, but here, it looks like they are mostly Gentiles.*" Even though I had protested silently in my heart, Judy and I became close friends that year. God was developing my character to mold me into the person He had created me to be.

My eighth grade science teacher at Jesse Ketchum made a strong impression on my memory. Because I was asked to sit up front, I was thought of as the "teacher's pet". A group of girls had a crush on Mr. Darnley. They thought he was cute with his blonde curly hair, large baby blue eyes, and gold rimmed glasses. One day, he produced a small garter snake and asked me to hold out my arm. I did and he promptly placed the creature on me. I went into silent shock as it started to crawl up my arm with its little tongue going in and out of its mouth faster than I could blink my eye. Mr. Darnley calmly explained how this was a harmless little creature and how I was such a good and brave student to sit quietly through this demonstration. He picked it up as it reached my shoulder and was almost eye to eye with me. My heart was pounding so hard I thought everyone could hear it even over the sound of Alice's voice, the pretty blonde at the back of the class, who was screaming at the top of her lungs.

One afternoon while I was attending Jesse Ketchum School, I was merrily walking home with a few schoolmates: Roberta from my street and a couple of boys. I was enjoying the cool fall air when suddenly, the bright, dancing sunlight turned dark for me as the conversation changed from movies and comic books to "those dirty Jews." At times like this I would use my acting skills to appear interested while in my silence, I felt like such a coward. I was never really sure if they knew that I was Jewish. I wanted to stand up for myself and my family but I was terrified. The kids at Jesse Ketchum were a much rougher bunch than what I was used to. Huron Street School was close to Brunswick Avenue and Kensington Market, an ethnic Jewish district at that time. But, Jesse Ketchum was located in a predominately Gentile area. I grew up with a haunting feeling that I didn't belong anywhere. There was a silent scream in my heart. It was a cry for help. It was a cry of who am I?

One of my favorite pastimes as a young teenager was to take long walks alone along the boardwalk on the Toronto Islands. The reverberation of foaming, icy cold waves crashing and whooshing against the rocks on the shore was comforting to me. Once again, as when I was a small child at Bubbie's cottage at Lake Simcoe, I immersed myself in fantasies of adventure and romance in faraway places.

In 1957, Larry took me to see the movie, "Bridge on the River Kwai" at the University Theater in Toronto. I remember that I felt so special that my oldest brother would want to take me to a movie, just the two of us. I had that same feeling when my brother Stan took me to a concert at Massey Hall, as he was a classical music fan. It is interesting to me now that one of Stan's most favorite pieces of classical music was "Handel's Messiah". This breathtakingly God inspired composition which is so full of Messianic prophecies and their fulfillment in our Jewish Messiah,

Chapter 6

Jesus, must surely have imparted the Truth into my brother's spirit as a young man.

Stan played the violin in high school, and I remember my father taking me to a concert at Harbord Collegiate High School. Stan was in the orchestra and even though I couldn't see him from the balcony, I was so proud to be his sister! He joined the Reserve Army while in high school and used to bribe my sister and me to polish his boots until we could see our faces in them. He was a regular Tom Sawyer. I'm surprised he never coerced us into white-washing the fence in our backyard.

Stan used to go off to army camp during the summers. We always knew when he was coming home for a visit because Mummy would be busy peeling apples and cooking them into a delicious, savory sauce for her Stanley. "Ma, why are you making applesauce today?" I would ask.

"Your brother's coming home tomorrow and you know that he loves applesauce."

"Esther, you don't know if your son is coming home tomorrow. He didn't send us a letter. We haven't heard anything!"

"Albert, mark my words, Stanley is coming home tomorrow." Mummy was always right. In fact, he often showed up the very night that she was cooking his favorite delight.

As the boxes raced towards me, I fumbled with my sweaty hands to try to wrap brown paper around them. The lady with the long red fingernails just kept sending box after box towards me. They were piling up and then tumbling off at the end of the belt line landing around my feet. *How did I ever get into this mess? I can't do this! I'm a complete failure. Daddy will be so disappointed in me because everyone knows that I'm 'Big Al's' daughter.'"* These thoughts were racing through my head as I tried my best to keep up. I was twelve years old, and would begin my first year at high school in the fall. My father had managed to get me a summer job at Rust Craft Greeting Cards where he worked as a lithographer.

Someone must have noticed my plight. A girl named Sam (short for Samantha) came alongside me and stayed until I caught on. I was amazed at how quickly I became dexterous at it once she demonstrated the technique to me. Sam was my age and it appeared that her only vision in life was to become a manager at that factory when she grew up. I remember thinking, *I'm going to get an education so I don't end up here for the rest of my life!*

Sam and I used to ride the streetcar home together after work. It was crowded, hot, steamy and smelly. Sam would always take out a Spanish onion from her pocket and eat it like an apple. I guess, along with the clammy, putrid odors being emitted from bodies jammed against each other in that hot, humid August air, the onion didn't stand out that much. "Rhonda, you should really try one of these," she insisted more than once. "I have an extra one if you like."

"No thanks," I always stammered, "I really prefer to eat apples but thanks just the same."

One thing was for certain in our lives. After my sister and I reached the age of 12 and 13, we never lacked for a fashionable winter coat. We often wore hand-me-down skirts and sweaters from our cousins that didn't fit us. Many of our other clothes were special bargains from a small, privately owned clothing establishment where Mummy would haggle for the prices as if we were at an open air bazaar in Europe. But we knew our coats would be top-of-the-line designer fashion! Mummy would get on the old black dial telephone each new winter season and call her brothers at the factory. She would tell them the girls need new winter coats again and we knew that our mother could pull it off. She was an expert negotiator! Often, I would hear her exclaim, "Yes, yes I know you just gave them a coat last year but the girls are growing like weeds! They can't even get into those old coats!"

So, the three of us would set out by bus and streetcar to go to Wilson Garments. I remember one particularly blustery winter

Chapter 6

day when it was snowing heavily and the icy wind was cutting into our faces like a sharp razor. We were standing on Queen Street waiting for the street car to arrive when Mummy said, "Wouldn't it be nice if one of your uncles came along now in their car?" Alas, they never did. I'm sure it was hard for her because she had terribly painful bunions on her feet and her shoes were stiff, uncomfortable oxfords. But, for Mummy, no sacrifice was too great for her girls.

From my mother, I learned to respect others; to have compassion and humility and to always be kind and generous no matter how people may treat you. She would say that there was always a reason why people were mean or inconsiderate. It was usually because they were so sad themselves and probably had no one to love them.

Matthew 25:34-36 Come, you blessed of My Father, inherit the kingdom prepared for you from the foundation of the world: for I was hungry and you gave Me food; I was thirsty and you gave Me drink; I was a stranger and you took Me in; I was naked and you clothed Me; I was sick and you visited Me; I was in prison and you came to Me.

I discovered a family secret as a young girl when my mother sent me to her room to bring her something or other from her dresser. As I was rummaging through the drawers to find it, I came across my father's birth certificate, of all things. I was shocked to read that the name on the document was "Abraham" and not "Albert." Later, when I questioned my father about it, he told me why he had changed his name. That was how I came to know about Daddy being called "Abie the Jew" when he was a child.

Shortly after that, I was let in on another secret when Mummy mentioned to me in a rather "matter of fact" way that Daddy had left her for a few years when Larry was perhaps three years old. She said that she cried so much to her family that she "wanted her Albert" that they brought him back to her. I know there was a rift between my mother's brothers and my father but I have no idea why he left her or how it was that they knew where he was to bring him back to his Esther.

After Daddy went away, Mummy and Larry were taken from their home in the tenement house to live with our Bubbie and Zaide Wilson as that was when Larry had rheumatic fever. Apparently, Aunt Bertha, being the youngest, was still at home when Larry and Mummy came to stay with our grandparents. My sister just recently told me that Larry says he remembers Uncle Will coming to the house to court Aunt Bertha.

CHAPTER 7

"You Don't Know Who He Is?!"

I was twelve years old when I started high school because of having combined three years into two during my elementary grades. My first year, I attended Harbord Collegiate, where my brother Stan had gone. There was a girl in my class whose name was Bambie. She told me that her family had given her that nickname because she had an Italian nanny when she was a baby who used to refer to her as "Little Bambino". We became close friends and decided to join the school band together. Bambie chose to play the French horn and I chose the trumpet. We rode the streetcar together after school and chattered endlessly about our trials and tribulations in high school. I often brought my trumpet home to practice in the basement of our house and the rest of the family had to endure hearing "Good Night Ladies" over and over. I enjoyed music and English and I think those were the only two subjects I passed in grade nine.

My English teacher, Mrs. Christian, really took an interest in me. One day, we had a discussion in class on the subject of Capital Punishment. I boldly made my feelings known that I was against putting anyone to death. Our teacher then instructed us to write an essay on the subject. I was passionate about it and set out with zeal to put my thoughts down on paper. I wrote in great detail about why I disagreed with Capital Punishment. The evening before I took my essay to school, I enthusiastically asked my father to take a look at what I had written. To my shock and horror he gave me his opinion of how we should not be feeding and housing murderers with our tax dollars and that I should change my essay. Unfortunately, I did change it to almost word for word from my father's lips.

Chapter 7

The next day in class, Mrs. Christian proudly asked me to read my work first. I knew what she was expecting and I literally felt sick to my stomach as I began to read because for one thing, I knew that my teacher would know it was a total lie. It was not my essay at all; it was my father's! As I hesitantly read out loud, my mother's words were ringing in my ears. *"Never forget, Rhonda, a little white lie will always turn into a big black lie. Even when it hurts, it is better to tell the truth."* When I finished reading, I couldn't bear the look of disappointment on Mrs. Christian's face. I learned a very important lesson that day—not to compromise the truth.

My high school science teacher at Harbord Collegiate had an impact on me just as my eighth grade science teacher at Jesse Ketchum had, not with a garter snake, but by starting me on a quest. I was once again at the front of the class, but this time because I couldn't read the black board. (I later had my eyes checked which resulted in the purchase of a pair of ugly black horn rimmed glasses for me to wear at school.) What stuck in my mind from this science teacher was that he emphatically told us that there was no such thing as absolute truth. He said that truth was ever changing so that we only believed something to be true until a scientific discovery would cause a new truth to emerge, thus making the first truth irrelevant. Something inside of me rebelled at this. *How could this be?* I pondered. *If that is so, there is no absolute—no anchor—to hold me or compass to guide me. It means that everything is constantly changing to fit a new reality. Surely, there must be an absolute truth in the universe somewhere!* I purposed in my heart to set out to find that truth.

After failing ninth grade at Harbord Collegiate, I switched to the same high school as my sister which was Northern Secondary, a commercial school consisting of grades nine through twelve. Harbord Collegiate was a "Matric School" (as it was called in those days) and went from grades nine to thirteen. If I had continued at Harbord Collegiate, after completing grade thirteen, I would have qualified for entrance to a university. But my father didn't believe that girls should seek higher education. He said they would only get married and have children, and all that time and money would be wasted. So, I took the easy road to avoid the humiliation of repeating grade nine at Harbord to start fresh at a new school. Years later, my business education from Northern Secondary proved to be very useful to me as a single mother. No matter where I lived, I was successful at finding employment.

At sixteen years old, I still knew very little about my mother's hospital stay until one evening when I was watching the movie, "Snake Pit," starring Olivia De Havilland, which was released by 20th Century Fox. It is about an outwardly normal young woman whose behavior gradually becomes erratic enough that her husband seeks professional help by having her committed to a psychiatric state hospital. I was glaring in shock into the television at what seemed to be a house of horrors in the asylum when my mother entered the room and watched with me for a bit. Then, as she continued on her way to the kitchen, she said in a rather nonchalant way, "That's just like the place that I was in."

I couldn't believe my ears. *Mummy was in an insane asylum?*

This information was incomprehensible to me. I had known she was sick, but I had always pictured her as being in a regular hospital. All I had known was that my father had insisted on taking her out of the hospital because she was refusing to eat and that he had to give her injections every day for a while after she came home.

I called out, "Mummy, what about the ice baths and the electric shock?" She yelled back from the kitchen that yes, she also had been forced to have those treatments. My mother returned, sat down beside me on the couch and told me calmly that when she was first committed, she was locked in a cell with a mad woman who used to burn my mother's arms with cigarette butts. Here I was, viewing unbelievably horrible, nightmarish scenes and my mother was casually commenting to me about her experience as if it was just a home video.

Chapter 7

My mother had the amazing gift of being able to exist in the realm of the present while leaving the past behind and holding onto hope for the future. It seems that she may have passed some of that on to me. I tucked the asylum information neatly into a safe compartment in my brain, a place that could be reached if needed, but far enough into the recesses of my mind so as not to disturb me.

My mother suffered severe grand mal epileptic seizures and debilitating migraine headaches for the rest of her life which I believed was caused by those primitive electric shock treatments that had been administered to her in the asylum. This was confirmed to me as a young woman when I questioned our family doctor about whether the epilepsy could be passed on to me. He told me, "Rhonda, you don't have to be concerned. The seizures that your mother suffers from are not hereditary."

When I made the decision to write this account of my life journey, I attempted to obtain some documentation of her hospital stay but was told that the records had long since been destroyed.

During my high school years Daddy was finally able to open his own art shop on Avenue Road which he named "Albert's Art Shoppe." It had been his hope for many years to be able to leave the factory and start his own business. I was happy for him being able to finally realize his dream. After Bubbie Wilson had died, my mother received a sum of money as an inheritance which she gave to her Albert for his Art Shoppe. I hold my mother in high esteem for the sacrifices that she made throughout her life for her husband and her family.

However, Daddy didn't have a lot of business savvy and, regrettably, went bankrupt. But, not before he personally met a few folk singers that were around in the 1960's like Bob Dylan, Peter, Paul, and Mary, and Gordon Lightfoot. His shop was on Avenue Road across the street from Yorkville which, in the 1960's, was a district of outdoor and indoor café's where people would gather to listen to rhythm and blues and folk music.

One summer, I worked as a waitress at a café while Sonny Terry and Brownie McGhee were performing. That is when I fell in love with the harmonica. It has that same deep, emotional draw for me as the faint melody of the distant clacking of the wheels of a train as it travels along the tracks in the quiet of the night. During the summer months, Avenue Road was bustling with activity. Many of the visiting musicians would wander into Albert's Art Shop while strolling along the boulevard. Daddy loved conversing with them and sometimes they even purchased a few art supplies or brought in a picture to be framed.

My brother Larry and I sometimes helped out at Daddy's store. I don't remember if Gilda or Stan did. That was when I recall my father advising me to be sure to save a little money from every paycheck, even if it was only a dollar. "After twenty years, it will add up," he used to say. He repeated this to the rest of us at various intervals.

I struggled with feelings of inadequacy and insecurity as a child and into my teen years. I never felt that I was perfect enough. I compared myself to other young girls and wished that I looked like them. One time in particular, I remember seeing the movie, "Gigi," when I was about twelve or thirteen years old. It was a 1958 musical and Gigi was played by Leslie Caron. I became completely absorbed in that film as I watched and experienced the emotions of young Gigi. I could absolutely relate to her whimsical personality and her dreams of love and marriage.

I longed to be transformed into an elegant woman the way it happened to her in the film. I remember wishing that I looked like her. I was never satisfied with my straight brunette hair or the shape of my legs, even though I was told by my father that I was a very pretty girl. Once when I was about fifteen years old, I was expressing that I thought I was ugly. "What do you mean ugly?" my father exclaimed. "Rhonda, you look just like Elizabeth Taylor!"

Chapter 7

He meant well but had said absolutely the wrong thing because at that time Elizabeth Taylor had put on quite a lot of weight.

"Oh Daddy, you think I'm fat, too!" I cried as I ran out of the house. I didn't know then about the Scripture, *And as the bridegroom rejoices over the bride, so shall your God rejoice over you* (Isaiah 62:5).*"*

I finished my four years of high school when I was seventeen. The one bright light during those difficult years was Mrs. Norris, my English teacher. She was an eccentric older lady with curly white hair and a pink bald spot in the middle of the top of her head. Mrs. Norris taught English in China during summer vacation and would always tell us, "Don't ever think that you will never go anywhere. You may very well find yourself in China one day, too." She was a great inspiration. She taught us to dream and have vision and really encouraged me in my writing.

Sadly, it was during my years at Northern Secondary that I believed a lie about myself. I went to the school counselor in grade nine and expressed a desire to go to college after high school. He told me to forget about it because my IQ test results showed that I would never qualify. I should have realized it could not possibly be the truth because in elementary school I had been put into the advanced stream to do second, third, and fourth grades in two years. Back then, in the school's opinion, I was considered to be scholastically above average for my age. But now in high school I was told that my IQ Test Scores did not even qualify for me to attend college!

I began to think that I must have become stupid as I was growing up. After all, I had failed grade nine at Harbord Collegiate and, on top of that I became clumsy, especially when I was nervous. Too many times I had been horribly embarrassed when running into class late and my books would slip from my arms to the floor capturing the attention of the whole class and the wrath of the teacher. So, as disappointing as this new setback was to me, I decided to make the best of it. From then on, after I had been told about my low IQ score, I was more interested in finding a boyfriend than doing homework. I did, however, excel in English and writing and enjoyed track and field. I even wanted to join the band but at that school, girls were only allowed to play instruments like the violin or flute, not a trumpet. So, I foolishly said, "If I can't play the trumpet, I won't play anything!"

It was in grade eleven that I was summoned to the counselor's office and told that they had made a terrible mistake in my first year and had gotten my IQ test results mixed up with someone else's. They apologized, but it was too late. I had lost all interest in school by that time. That is how powerful a lie can be if you choose to believe it. *"And you shall know the truth and the truth will set you free"* (John 8:32). We can choose to believe a lie or we can choose to believe the truth.

I muddled my way through the rest of high school while working as an usher and a popcorn/candy attendant at a couple of different movie theatres. I also found employment as a sales assistant in the old Woolworth's Department store on Bloor Street in Toronto. In addition, I held down a long term part-time job at Cole's Book Stores during those years which turned out to be my favorite. I loved being amongst the books that, to me, held many fascinating adventures and secrets about life. I especially liked the yellow smock that I had to wear to identify me as a store clerk. I suppose it gave me a feeling of importance.

It was while working at Coles Book Store on Bloor Street that I became friends with a Greek girl named Christina. She was a fellow employee and as we talked with each other on our breaks, we found out that we both loved to ride horses. Sometimes I took the streetcar to Christina's house on the weekends and her mother always insisted that I must be Greek! My long, straight black hair, hazel eyes and olive complexion caused more than one person in that neighborhood to think that I was Greek. I didn't mind, as I really did not want to be known as *the Jewish girl*.

Chapter 7

Christina and I used to go horseback riding together at a commercial stable somewhere in her area of the city. We were led by a guide on trails through the woods for an hour. One time, I was given a really old mare to ride. When we came to a sandy patch of ground, that old mare just got down on her knees and, before I knew it, she started to roll over on her side to scratch her back in the sand. I managed to free my feet from the stirrups and jump off just in time. I was going to walk back to the stables but the young man who was the trail guide insisted that I get right back on that horse. "If you don't get on now, you will be afraid to ever get on a horse again. She's just a tired old horse. Don't worry. I'll get her to keep going for you." I reluctantly mounted my trusty steed once more. Then, after making sure that I was securely in my saddle, he took a lit cigarette butt and pressed it into the horse's rear end. She took off like the wind and galloped back to the stables, arriving there before anyone else. I was glad to have been encouraged to conquer my fear but I was very upset at the way that young man treated that tired old horse. Once again, angels were watching over me.

One summer, I landed a position as a typist at the office of the Professional Engineers of Ontario which was in the Church of the Messiah building at the end of our street. It was in that same church building where I had been turned away when I attempted to join "Brownies" at the age of seven. As I was being interviewed for the job, I just answered, "Yes, I know how to do that" to just about anything that they asked me. So, after working there for about one week during the summer, one of the secretaries passed by my desk and noticed that my basket was full of carbon papers. My cover was blown! It was obvious that I had never used carbon paper in a typewriter before and I just threw away each sheet after using it once. (We were not in the computer age yet!)

I will never forget the women in that office. They took me under their wing and taught me everything I needed to know about office work. I suppose you could say that I had chutzpa because that became a normal procedure for me in years to come. I would say that I could do the job and then I would learn it as I went along.

While attending Northern Secondary High School, I was introduced to Fred by my Jewish friend Barbara. She had asked me to babysit with her one Saturday night. When I arrived at her house, her parents were not at home but there were no children to watch. "What's going on?" I asked.

"Don't worry, I can explain" replied Barbara a little sheepishly. The next thing I knew, the doorbell rang and in walked Barbara's boyfriend, Seymour, and another fellow, Fred. Barbara and Seymour quickly disappeared into another room leaving me alone with Fred. This was obviously a set-up. When I asked Fred to take me home, he graciously obliged. I felt like a complete fool! Fred was eighteen and I was fifteen years old. He was in his first year at the University of Toronto studying to become a lawyer. I do not recall discussing anything about this surprise date with my parents or brothers.

I thought that I would never hear from Fred again but he called and invited me to a fraternity party. The only party dress that I owned was turquoise blue chiffon with puffy sleeves and a large band around the waist that tied in a bow at the back. It must have been one of the hand-me-downs that Aunt Bertha and Aunt Lil dropped off on occasion from our cousins, Joanne and Linda. Fred arrived at our house to escort me to the party. He was extremely well mannered as he commented, with his dark brown eyes popping out of their sockets, "You sure look, umm, nice. Let's go."

When we arrived at the house, I saw the girls coming along the street with their dates to go to the party. I was already out of my league because they were all university students. It was during the beatnik years and they were wearing basic black or grey knit sweaters, wool stockings and short, tight skirts. "Please, take me home," I pleaded. "I can't go in there." Fred insisted that I looked

Chapter 7

pretty and that because he was with me it didn't matter how the other girls were dressed. There was a lot of heckling from the other male fraternity members but Fred held up very well. Even though I felt humiliated, I was impressed with how Fred was so protective of me.

Fred told me that he didn't mind if I dated other boys but if I ever dated a Gentile, it would be the end of our relationship. After we had been going out together for a couple of months, Fred took me to meet his parents who were Holocaust survivors. They did not approve of me. They felt that since my parents did not keep a kosher home that I was not suitable for him and, in any case, they had their eyes on the girl across the street for their son.

When his parents told me that we must never forget the Holocaust, I had no concept of what they meant. I had not even read *The Diary of Anne Frank* and had no knowledge of the incomprehensible horrors of which they were speaking. It was not until I was in my twenties that I viewed a documentary on television about the atrocities of the Hitler years. I have recently devoured several books on the subject. I have much admiration and gratitude for those Holocaust survivors who were brave enough to face the fear of reliving their pain by recounting in writing what they and their families personally endured.

Around the age of fifteen while I was still dating Fred and trying to fit in with his older, more educated crowd, I developed an anxiety disorder. I guess you could call it a type of agoraphobia. After going to a movie, Fred and I were having coffee in a restaurant with some of his university friends. They began a political conversation about Haile Selassie, the well known Emperor of Ethiopia, who had gone to the League of Nations in 1936 to condemn the use of chemical weapons by Italy against his people. As soon as the name "Haile Selassie" was mentioned, I piped up loudly and asked, "Who's Haile Selassie?"

Suddenly, all eyes were upon me and, as if in a chorus that had been rehearsed previously, everyone exclaimed in astonished unison, "You don't know who Haile Selassie is?!" Immediately, a hot flush started with a burning sensation from my belly right up to my face. I sat dumbfounded. Fred quickly steered the conversation in another direction as I attempted to appear casual. As I nervously lifted my coffee to my lips, my neck began to twitch. I was afraid that I wouldn't be able to hold my head still enough to drink. I quickly returned my cup to the table before anyone would notice the twitching. My fear of others noticing that something was wrong with me was more powerful than the phobia itself. That incident was the beginning of a battle with anxiety attacks that continued for the next thirty years.

The second attack took place when I was at the hair salon having my hair styled with one of those bouffant looks where my long black hair would be piled in large curls on top of my head. Suddenly, as I sat looking into the mirror while the hairdresser was staring at me to see how high to pile my hair, I felt as if my neck was going to start twitching, and I broke out in a cold sweat. I stiffened my body trying as hard as I could to control my nerves. It was so noticeable that the hairdresser asked, "What's wrong? Are you feeling sick? Can I get you a little water to drink, dear?"

"Oh. No thanks." I shakily replied. "I'll just go home to bed. I must be coming down with the flu or something."

"But, I haven't finished setting your hair!" she exclaimed. I just slid off the chair, asked her how much I needed to pay her, and ran out of there as fast as I could. I am not sure if I ever went back to that same hair salon after that.

I never knew when these attacks were going to come. Usually, it would be in a place where either the attention was on me or where I was in the midst of a large crowd such as at a concert or a theater. It was worse if I was sitting in an auditorium with a very high ceiling.

I never told anyone in my family because of my mother's history and the fear that I would be sent away to some institution from the dark ages. Even though my sister and I grew up as close

Chapter 7

as two sisters could possibly be, I never told her. I attended many concerts at Massey Hall in Toronto with Gil when we were in our late teens. During every concert, I would battle inwardly to keep myself from having an attack. It took intense concentration and I could only relax when it was finally time to get up and leave the concert hall.

I continued a relationship with Fred for a couple of years until I broke the news to him one night that I was going to date a Gentile boy named Tom. That was "Goodbye Fred." I was seventeen, working as a candy bar attendant at the old Imperial movie theater in downtown Toronto, when I met Tom. My sister already had a part time job there. We worked together selling popcorn and candy and watching movies for free on our breaks. Thereafter, I did not relish eating popcorn at movie theaters after seeing that they dumped the unused popcorn into huge bins to be reheated the next day in the "popper" to look as if it was freshly popped!

At that time, the Imperial Theater was an imposing structure with a magnificent high domed ceiling and elegant gold leaf and marble balconies. (As palatial as it was, for some reason, I do not remember ever having to fight anxiety attacks while there. Perhaps, it was because I was so busy, plus I was absolutely infatuated with Tom.) The theater, originally named "Pantages" in 1920, had seating to accommodate over three thousand people, making it one of the largest theaters in the country. In 1972 it became "Imperial Six", having been remodeled to a six screen multiplex. It was closed for a while and has now been re-converted to a live theater using its original name "Pantages".

Tom was of Estonian background, tall with fair skin, blonde hair, and blue eyes that were too small for my liking but I was drawn to his gentle personality. We dated for a couple of years and one summer I nursed him through a terrible bout of chicken pox.

One winter, Tom and I decided to try downhill skiing. Neither of us had ever attempted it before, so, with much excitement and anticipation, we went downtown to purchase our equipment. We both bought blue skis and I could hardly wait to use them. I invited my Polish girlfriend Helena to come along and Tom invited a young man who was an acquaintance of his. I don't remember his name but he was the only one in our group who could ski. We all piled into Tom's blue Pontiac and drove to Toronto's Don Valley slopes. There were three hills, each one a little steeper than the other. So we decided to try the easiest one first which was straight downhill to the bottom. After taking the chair lift to the top, I was anxious to be the most daring by skiing down the hill before my friends.

It was a crisp, cold day and the brilliant white snow was glistening like little diamonds in the sun. *How hard can this be?* I thought. I pushed off with my poles and only then noticed that I was not alone on this hill. There were so many skiers and it seemed that they were all in front of me. I had no idea how to turn or navigate my way around anyone.

There was nothing to do but shout, "Excuse me, excuse me! I'm a new skier!" I can still see those people, heads turning and then fleeing out of my way. It was a miracle that I managed to ski to the bottom without crashing into anyone and somehow swerve my body to the left in order to avoid going straight through the fence at the end of the ski run! Helena saw me pull this off so she tried it too and, unfortunately, she crashed into that fence. Thankfully, it was only a flimsy snow fence and she was not injured.

One evening, Tom took me out to eat at a Chinese restaurant and then to dance at a disco club in Yorkville. While dancing, my eyes began to feel irritated and puffy so I went to the ladies' room to take a look. Of course, the lighting was so dim that I could not see anything so I just assumed that my eye makeup was bothering me. I went back upstairs and as we started to dance, Tom said in a very calm voice, "We have to leave right now."

"Why?"

"I'll tell you when we get to the car."

Chapter 7

We got into his blue Pontiac and he drove me straight to the emergency room of Toronto General Hospital without saying a word. By the time we arrived, my face was feeling like the skin was pulling really tight, and my throat was closing up so that it was difficult to swallow. As we entered the emergency area, I noticed that people were staring at me. We reached the reception desk where the clerk refused to admit me because I did not have my OHIP (Ontario Health Insurance Plan) card with me. Thanks be to God, a nurse came by at that moment and exclaimed, "What did you *eat?*" She hurried me to a cubicle and instructed me to disrobe and that was when I got really scared. My body was covered with gigantic red hives. The doctor immediately came and injected me with a shot of adrenaline and told me not to get up.

I asked the nurse, "Does my face look really bad?"

She replied, "Well, not having seen you before, I can't really say." It turned out that I had experienced an acute allergic reaction known as anaphylaxis from something I had eaten. I went to my own doctor the next day, and he was furious that the hospital had not kept me overnight.

I was living a life that was quickly heading for destruction. Yet, with His unfathomable, unquenchable love, God showed me mercy over and over again. How many times had I begged Him crying, "Oh please God, don't let me be pregnant this time and I promise that I will never sleep with another boy again until I am married!" I broke my promise time after time and my unfaithfulness was to eventually catch up with me.

Romans 5:8 *But God demonstrates His own love toward us, in that while we were still sinners, Christ died for us.*

Romans 6:23 *For the wages of sin is death, but the gift of God is eternal life in Christ Jesus our Lord.*

CHAPTER 8

"Don't Worry. We Can Take Care Of This."

After finishing high school at Northern Secondary, I set out on my search for full time employment. Interviews were an interesting experience. Each interview inevitably led to the same question. With the last name of Middlestadt, I was repeatedly asked the same question, "What are you?"

I would reply, "I am Canadian."

The interviewer would say, "But, really, what nationality are you? Are you German or Dutch?"

"I am Canadian but my name is of German and Dutch descent." I always suspected that they were searching to find out if I was Jewish, and I was determined not to give them that information. Even though this was the 1960's, there was still strong evidence of anti-Semitism in Toronto.

> "Throughout the 1930's and 1940's, employment discrimination against Jews in Canada was rampant. During this time, there were racial prohibitions that stopped Jews from becoming lawyers, pharmacists, miners, loggers, or fishermen and denied them minimum wage rights and welfare benefits. Typical employment applications asked for racial origin and religion, and if a Jew was inadvertently hired by misrepresentation, he or she could be fired. There were few to none Jewish teachers, professors, architects, principals, engineers or accountants. Many institutions maintained quotas on how many Jews they would hire, or hired none at all (such as the City of Toronto, who refused to hire Jewish police officers and transit workers). Often owners and managers tried to deflect them by putting up signs with slogans such as "Gentiles Only," or "No Jews or Dogs Allowed" ("Anti-Semitism in Canada," Wikipedia, the free encyclopedia).

Chapter 8

My sister and I left home when I was eighteen and she was seventeen. By that time, my brothers had both moved out and our father had sold our house on Dupont Street. My father, mother, sister, and I moved together into a two bedroom apartment on Spadina Avenue. The change for my mother was overwhelming. First of all, the apartment had an electric stove which she had never used before, but more than that, Dupont Street had been like a small village with friends dropping by for tea or gathering on one another's front porches to chat. Apartment living was totally different with its elevators and dimly lit, empty hallways. I am sure that my mother felt isolated there. It was also a challenge for Gil and me. We had to share a very small bedroom. Our Aunts Lil and Bertha came over to help us *get organized*. Their expert advice to us was, "You just need to learn to consolidate your belongings."

The day Gil and I moved out, Mummy was standing in the doorway of our apartment wearing her house dress and apron with arms hanging down at her sides. Her curly dark hair framed a distraught face with tears glistening in those beautiful hazel eyes as she said, "Albert, what's going to happen to the girls?"

I felt a choking lump in my throat. As we left, I turned for one last glimpse of Mummy and said, "Don't worry, we won't be far away." Then we were out the door.

Actually, that first move only took us down the street, and I saw more of my mother after moving out than when I had lived at home. I frequently went to have a home cooked meal with Mom. Gil proved to be more prudent and wise with her finances than me. When I was short of money, I didn't want to be taking advantage of my younger sister. Besides, I really did miss my mom.

We lived near St. George and Bloor Streets in the basement apartment of a big old house which was close to the University of Toronto and Rochdale College.

> Opened in 1968, Rochdale College was an experiment in student-run alternative education and co-operative living in Toronto, Canada. It provided space for 840 residents in a co-operative living space. It was also a free university where students and teachers would live together and share knowledge. The project ultimately failed when it could not cover its financing and neighbors complained that it had become a haven for drugs and crime. It was closed in 1975 ("Rochdale College," Wikipedia, the free encyclopedia).

The next place that Gil and I shared was on the first floor of another rambling old house on Walmer Road, only a couple of streets over from our first apartment. I had long, black hair and dressed in such a way as to cause people to think I was part of the drug culture at Rochdale. Drugs were really of no interest to me at all. I tried marijuana once and it was as distasteful to me as trying to smoke a cigarette.

A childhood friend of ours who, unfortunately, had become involved with drugs and drug dealers asked me one day if I was "cool."

I replied, "Sure, I'm cool."

She said, "No, I mean are you really cool?"

I said, "Of course, I'm *really* cool."

I had no idea what she had meant by "cool" and that she was speaking in code for "Do you do drugs?" She proceeded to tell me that she and a couple of guys were going to take a ride to a small airport that night and they needed another girl to come along with them. It still amazes me that I was so naïve. Apparently, they were going to pick up a shipment of drugs and did not want to look suspicious. My friend told me the address where I was to meet them that evening. I was thinking this was going to be a fun double date, so I went.

The first thing that happened when I entered the house was that there was a large dish of multi colored pills in the middle of the coffee table. I sat down and started to reach forward to take

Chapter 8

a hand full as I thought that they were candies. I kid you not; I really did think they were candies. My friend screamed, "Ronnie, what are you doing? Don't you know those are psychedelic drugs?"

At the same time as she shouted, a young man with a pistol walked into the room. I suddenly realized that I was in a serious situation here. So, of course I replied, "Oh, I was just joking. You know me. I'm cool."

The guy asked her, "Are you sure she's cool?" Boy, I was really scared now.

We proceeded to pile into a small Volkswagen and I remember there was a large dog with us as we drove to some small airport. We waited for a very long time in the dark which seemed like hours to me. By the grace of God, the dealers they were waiting for never showed up, so instead of going home, they drove to a motel where we all stayed in the same room for the night. To this day, the only thing I remember about that room was seeing cartoons of Mickey Mouse over and over. It reminded me of when I was a small child and had to have two teeth pulled and was given laughing gas to make me sleep. It seemed to me that I saw the same Mickey Mouse cartoons then too.

I don't know for sure whether my friend and her buddies had slipped something into my coffee that night, but it is very likely that they did. It is one of those times that I know without a shadow of a doubt that God was looking out for me in my incredible foolishness.

It came out in the news not too many weeks later that the very house that I had gone to meet them in had been raided by the police and busted. The house was full of drugs and weapons and there were bullet holes in the basement walls. When I talked with my sister about the incident, she could not believe how I could have been so incredibly stupid as to get involved in something like that. It took some time to convince her that I really didn't know what was going on. I don't think she ever really believed me.

Shortly after that, Gil and I grew apart from each other and found separate living quarters. I was fast becoming a "Wandering Jew" in my search for meaning in my life. I rented a room in a house somewhere in the Ramsden Park area. There, I met a young man named Jamie who was from a small town in Southern Ontario. He had come to Toronto to look for work and rented a room down the hall from me. We would get together at night to play chess and we became good friends. Jamie was a huge fan of James Brown, the recording artist, so we went to one of his concerts at the Masonic Temple on Yonge Street. That turned out to be a most frightening experience for me. Near the end of the performance, we made our way to the front just below the stage. Everyone else had the same idea, and I felt that I was being crushed against the platform by hundreds of people. I don't remember how we managed to get out of there, but I never went to another rock concert after that. Once again, I'm sure God's angels were watching out for me!

Jamie and I decided to pool our resources and move together into a small apartment in a rambling old house in the Rosedale area of Toronto. That way, I would have a kitchen to cook in and not have to live on burgers and fries from "Harvey's Fast Food Restaurant." It was while residing there that I had a traumatic experience on my way home from work one evening. It was in October and was already dark as I walked from the subway along the street to our house. Suddenly, as I passed a wooded area, a short bald man came out of the dark behind me and pulled me down into a pile of leaves. I must have glanced back for a few seconds. That is the only explanation I have of how I knew he was short and bald. I had my umbrella with me, but I dropped it and started screaming at the top of my lungs. He had just gotten his hand between my legs when I heard the clicking of high heels running towards me. The little man ran away and when I got home, I called the police. Mini skirts were in fashion and I had on a short red and white plaid skirt. I never wore the really short minis

Chapter 8

because I was self conscious about my legs, so this one fell just to the top of my knees. When the policeman arrived, the first thing he asked me after I shakily related the details to him about being attacked was, "Is *that* what you were wearing when it happened?" His condemning tone of voice made me feel that he was blaming *me* for the incident. He half heartedly said they would look for the perpetrator. "Would you like to press charges if we find him?" he asked me.

"No, don't bother," I ashamedly replied. By this time, I just wanted to be left alone. If they ever found the man, I was never told.

I didn't get much support from Jamie either. He just said, "Hey, it's not such a big deal. You didn't get hurt. My mother was attacked once and *she* didn't get into a big panic about it." So, I didn't bother to tell anyone else. Before that, I had never given any thought to jogging at night. Now, I became very aware of anyone walking behind me on the street, even in the daytime.

Inevitably, Jamie and I developed an intimate relationship. One day, he decided that he wanted to see the world and left. After Jamie had been gone for about a month, I realized that I was pregnant. I called his buddies and asked them if they knew where he was. They said they had no idea, that he probably was somewhere in the United States. I had the feeling that he had told them not to let me know. I was too afraid to tell them I was pregnant. I was around twenty years old and did not know where to turn. I finally mustered up enough courage to call my father and give him the news. He said, "Don't worry, we can take care of this, but under no circumstance, are you to tell your mother."

I had no idea what *take care of this* meant until I met my father at a restaurant with a doctor that he had called. He explained to the doctor that his daughter had gotten herself in trouble and asked him how much money would be needed to *take care of it*. There was that phrase again and slowly, I was beginning to realize what was taking place, but as I often did in situations where I felt helpless, I froze in silence like a cold stone statue while my future was being decided for me. After the good doctor left, my father again made it very clear that I was not to tell my mother about this as it would kill her.

Later, I wished that I had talked to my mother because I knew she was the one person who would have stopped me from doing the unthinkable. We all have a choice, but once again, I chose to listen to a lie rather than listening to what God was telling me in my heart. I knew that I was carrying a gift of new life but I listened to the voices that were screaming at me and telling me that I had no choice, that this was what I had to do. At that time, abortion was illegal in Canada. A place and time was set up where I was to meet with the doctor. When he arrived, he told me to sit on what was a dining room table and wait. He had said it was good that I was not yet in my seventh week of pregnancy because after that, it would be wrong to do it. Somehow, that didn't make sense to me.

Jeremiah 1:5 *"Before I formed you in the womb, I knew you."*

Psalm 139:13-16 *For You formed my inward parts;*
You covered me in my mother's womb.
I will praise You, for I am fearfully and wonderfully made;
Marvelous are Your works,
And that my soul knows very well.
My frame was not hidden from You,
When I was made in secret,
And skillfully wrought in the lowest parts of the earth.
Your eyes saw my substance, being yet unformed.
And in Your book they all were written,
The days fashioned for me,
When as yet there were none of them.

I sat transfixed and paralyzed with fear as I watched the doctor take his instruments out of his bag and set them on white cloths on the counter. I wanted to shout *"STOP!"* and run out of that house but somehow I was glued to the spot, trembling. My heart

CHAPTER 8

was breaking with the knowledge of what was going to take place. From somewhere deep inside of me came a silent scream of, *"Help me; please help me."* But no help came. After what seemed like an eternity, the doctor began and when I started to cry out in agony he gave me a pillow to put over my face so the neighbors wouldn't hear. The physical pain was intense but the emotional pain was unbearable and inconsolable. I had never read the Bible but God had written His laws on my heart and I knew that I had just murdered my baby.

Hebrews 8:10 *For this is the covenant that I will make with the house of Israel after those days, says the Lord: I will put My laws in their mind and write them on their hearts; and I will be their God, and they shall be My people.*

Oh God, what have I done?! I cried out in my heart. I had just committed the most inconceivable act that I thought impossible for me to do. I abhorred and despised myself. Feeling that I no longer deserved to live, I waited for God's punishment to fall upon me. This would be the first time in my life that I felt completely hopeless.

Psalms 38:6 *I am troubled, I am bowed down greatly; I go mourning all the day long.*

Psalms 51:1-3 *Have mercy upon me, O God, According to Your lovingkindness; According to the multitude of Your tender mercies, Blot out my transgressions. Wash me thoroughly from my iniquity, And cleanse me from my sin. For I acknowledge my transgressions, And my sin is always before me.*

Psalms 34:18 *The LORD is near to those who have a broken heart, And saves such as have a contrite spirit.*

Don't Worry, We Can Take Care Of This

Wandering, Wondering Jew

CHAPTER 9

"I Could Use Some Good News!"

There I was, feeling lost, worthless, and without direction. I went once more to live with my sister. However, shortly after my arrival, I left again. I wrote Gil a note and boarded a bus to some city in Ontario. It didn't matter to me where I went. I just wanted to get away not only from Toronto, but from myself. I think I ended up in Kitchener and as I walked along the main street, I could have been anywhere as I was totally absorbed in my sorrow. That was when I met the future father of my two children. I will call him "R". R and I shared meals and stories together, except I did not tell him about the abortion. That was my dark secret. He told me how, when he was a young teenager, his parents had shipped him off from Italy to live with his relatives in Canada. He arrived not knowing a word of English. I was enamored by his sense of adventure. I also thought that he was quite handsome with his dark, wavy hair and huge brown eyes. He suggested we go to stay with his Aunt and Uncle in Sault Ste. Marie, Ontario where we could both find work. I had been living at the YWCA and had not been successful at job hunting in this small city, so I agreed.

His relatives were wonderful people and made me feel like part of the family right away. The only thing was, as part of their family, there were very strict rules of conduct for women. They were from the south of Italy or "the old country" as they referred to it. I was not allowed to go anywhere by myself, not even the library. I allowed myself to be controlled like this, I suppose, because I was in such great need of some kind of order and security in my life. I had no trouble finding employment, first as a sales clerk at a K-Mart store and then as a secretary in an insurance company.

Chapter 9

I phoned home to my sister to give her the good news so she wouldn't worry about me, but she didn't sound too happy. I can't blame Gil for being concerned about me as my behavior was obviously irrational. Nothing I told her would convince her that I shouldn't come right back home. But, nothing could convince me to return to the place where the unthinkable had taken place. In my mind, it was no longer "home" for me. So, I receded into my imaginary world of belonging to a happy family and I stayed with R. His family spoke Italian most of the time enabling me to pick up a few words and phrases here and there.

Sault Ste. Marie is in Northern Ontario about an eight and a half hour drive from Toronto. My first winter there was enchanting with the deep pure white snow that covered the landscape like a heavy blanket. Oh, how I wanted that pure white snow to erase my past sins.

The family felt we should be married so we arranged with the local Priest for a very small ceremony at a Catholic Church. I had never been in a Catholic church before and I didn't even know how to make the sign of the cross on myself. We went to see the Priest before we were married as I had already told the family that I was Jewish. I honestly do not remember what was discussed at that meeting. I wore a short red dress with white polka dots for the ceremony, not a wedding gown. There were only the two of us and two witnesses, being good friends of R, who later became the God parents of our daughter.

I was so absorbed in running away from my past that I didn't even tell my parents about my marriage until afterwards. While we were still living with R's aunt and uncle, I told him about the abortion. I was not prepared for the tirade of judgment and condemnation that came from him. This mortified me and I went into a deep despair. Not wanting to go on living, I took every pill that I could find in the medicine cabinet. As I was lying on the bed waiting to die I didn't even feel sleepy. It was not working at all so I decided to tell the family what I had done and they rushed me to the emergency room at the local hospital. The nurses told me to stick my finger down my throat so I could throw up the pills. They didn't know who they were telling this to. If there was ever anything I dreaded in my life, it was to throw up. I had managed to grow up relatively free from that experience as opposed to my sister who vomited on a regular basis. They finally threatened to pump my stomach, describing in gruesome detail what it would be like. That did it. I stuck my finger down my throat and out came all the pills!

Once again, God's unfathomable mercy was evident in my life.

We moved to our own place which really was just a bedroom, a kitchen and a bathroom on the second floor of a house owned by another Italian family. I became pregnant right away and nine months later gave birth to a perfectly healthy, beautiful baby girl. We named her Giuseppina Lisa. I later called her Josie. How overwhelming is God's grace to have allowed me to become a mother after what I had done. Arriving home from the hospital with Josie, I remember being enthralled holding this tiny, delicate bundle in my arms as I sat on the edge of my bed. I was overcome with love for her as I gazed at this new little person in amazement for quite some time before laying her carefully into the bassinette.

When Josie was about six months old, my sister brought my parents up to Sault Ste. Marie to see their first grandchild. By this time I was pregnant with my second child, Giuseppe Carlo (later called Carl). As I stood at the top of the stairs and saw them at the bottom, they appeared to me to have aged quite a lot. My father was thin and frail having had a stroke during that year with the result that his hair had instantly turned from black to white. My mother had let her hair grow long and had died it auburn. *Could these two strangers be my parents?*

Of course, I was glad to see them, but I was still feeling guilty about running off and getting married so our visit was rather tense

Chapter 9

as I remember it. Gil's friend Don had driven them up to the Sault. Since we had no room for them to sleep with us, they all stayed overnight in a hotel before driving back to Toronto. My life had changed so much since I had left Toronto that I felt like we were from different planets.

My son, Giuseppi Carlo (Carl), was born exactly one year after my daughter, almost to the day. Josie's birth date being October 28, 1971 and Carl's being October 29, 1972. While we were having a cake and a little birthday party for Josie turning one, I felt labor pains beginning. When my children were growing up I used to tell them that Carl had enjoyed a piece of Josie's first birthday cake while he was still in my tummy.

The next day, we were to have Josie baptized at the Catholic Church but when I woke up that morning, I felt the labor pains coming closer together. I didn't want to miss the baptism so I didn't say anything. At the church, the Priest took one look at my belly and asked me, "When are you due?"

I replied, "Any moment."

"Please, sit down, sit down," he said hastily. He rushed through the baptism and my husband, my daughter, the two God parents and I went out for lunch.

For some reason, I remember that I ate fish and when we were finished I said, "You better take me to the hospital. I am going to have my baby." No one would believe that I was about to give birth because I was so calm but I became adamant that I be taken to the hospital immediately.

Upon arriving at the General Hospital I was met with the same skepticism by the nurses. They insisted that I did not look like I was about to give birth until they put me on the examining table, took one look and exclaimed frantically, "Oh my goodness, she's having her baby. Get the doctor! Hurry!"

So, a perfectly healthy, handsome baby boy came into the world. I panicked when I realized that my baby had been taken away from me after his birth. I was assured by the nurses that everything was fine but since my son had been born breathing a little too fast, he was in an incubator for now. On the second day, I got up out of my bed, marched to the nursery, and insisted that they let me hold my baby! I would not leave until they did so. My newborn clutched tightly to me as I snuggled him closely against my breast. It was as though he was crying out, "Please don't let them take me from you, Mommy!" It was emotionally very difficult to return to my room without him as I was overwhelmed with love for him as I was with his sister when she was born. I went to him every day after that and held him for a while until he was able to be brought to me like the other babies.

Just before our son was born, we moved to a slightly larger apartment on the second floor of another house which had two bedrooms, a bathroom and a kitchen. After we brought Carl home, R decided that he wanted to take our daughter to Italy for a week so that his parents could see their grandchild. So, off they went and Josie became a world traveler at the tender age of one!

When they returned, we applied and were accepted into Ontario Housing (which is also called Low Income Housing). The two storey townhouses were designed in a circle with a courtyard in the center. I was thankful that now, I would not have to wash diapers by hand as there was a laundry room available on the premises. My next door neighbor was a single mom whose husband had left her with two children to raise on her own. This woman was very bitter and angry about her situation in life. I remember asking God to please not let me become like her. I was soon to find out the significance of that prayer.

One day, out of the blue, R told me that he wanted to move us to Winnipeg, Manitoba, about 700 miles or a sixteen hour drive away, where he would have an opportunity to find better employment. The only thing available to him in Sault Ste. Marie was to work at the Algoma Steel plant or as a cook in a restaurant. The plan was that he would get a job and a place for us to live and then come back for me and the children. As far as I knew, I had no reason not to believe him.

Chapter 9

While he was gone, I received our phone bill and it was for more than $100.00 which was out of the ordinary. I noticed a whole list of long distance calls that had been made. I assumed that there had been some error so I called the phone company. They checked and assured me that these calls had indeed been made from our phone.

I was still not suspicious as I thought that R might have been searching for work outside of the Sault. I decided to call one of the numbers listed which was in Winnipeg. I got the surprise of my life when a young woman answered and said she was the sister of the girl that my husband was living with! He later called me and made it very clear that he was leaving me and that I should go to the government and apply for welfare as he had no money to send to me. He was also very angry with me for interfering with his life.

I was in shock but I knew that I had to be strong and deal with my situation immediately. It was the beginning of winter and I had my two babies to take care of. I did not have the desire or energy to be angry with him or jealous of his girlfriend. I did wonder how I could have been so stupid as to not have suspected anything when he used to stay out all night saying that he had worked the late shift at the restaurant. All I know is, that after many tears, I dried my eyes, took a deep breath, and did what I always had done. I just put one foot in front of the other, one day at a time with the hope that tomorrow would be better than today.

Proverbs 14:30 *A sound heart is life to the body, But envy is rottenness to the bones.*

I felt too embarrassed and ashamed to call my family in Toronto to ask for help and I was afraid to contact R's family, thinking that they might try to take my children away from me. They were kind to me while we lived in their home, but they had never been too happy about the fact that I was Jewish. I thought to myself, "*There's no telling what they might do if they think the children might not be brought up as Catholics.*" When my sister would phone me to ask how we were, I did not let on that anything was amiss. That Christmas, two ladies showed up at my door with toys and gifts for the children and food for us. I was taken aback by their thoughtfulness and I never did find out who they were. They might have been from a local church or perhaps the Salvation Army. I may have been placed on a list of needy families as I had applied for and was receiving government assistance by that time.

I was with my daughter Josie in a bookstore on my way to the cash register, when a book on the bottom shelf of the isle I was passing caught my eye. It was as if someone was telling me to stop a moment and take a look at it. I stopped, picked it up and saw that the title was *Good News for Modern Man*. I thought, "*I could use some good news right about now.*" But then, I put it back on the shelf. While I was at the checkout counter, I had a very strong impression to go back and get the book. So, I did just that and purchased it.

When I got home, I could hardly wait until after I had put my children to bed to read it. To my complete surprise, when I opened it, it turned out to be a Bible! It was the New Testament and my immediate reaction was, "*I can't read this. This is the New Testament! I'm Jewish. Jews are not supposed to read the New Testament.*" I quickly closed it. But I had a nagging feeling that I *should* read it, and I also thought that perhaps I might find some answers as to who this Jesus was that I had wondered about since childhood. So, I opened to the beginning.

As I began the Book of Matthew, I saw in the genealogy that Jesus was indeed a Jew just as my mother had told me. He was listed as the son of Abraham, the son of Isaac, the son of Jacob. Even though I had never actually been taught about the Jewish Patriarchs, I had every so often peeked into the large black Old Testament that my father had purchased from a traveling salesman

Chapter 9

who had come to our house. Some statements that Jesus made reminded me of my mother; such as when He spoke about loving your neighbor, or of forgiveness and blessing your enemies. I was also excited to see that Jesus was a healer, just as Mummy had said. *"If this Jesus could see into men's hearts as the Scripture stated,"* I thought, *"perhaps, He could see into my heart, too."* I just knew that somehow, He held the key, the answer for my life. I saw that Jesus triumphed over death, that the grave could not hold him! I became absorbed in the Book of Matthew and read it from start to finish. Whenever I had a quiet moment during the next few months, I went through it again and again.

I experienced supernatural emotional healing and peace that I had not yet known in my life. I can't say that I understood with my mind what I was reading but I understood with my heart. It was from the Holy Spirit to my spirit. I believe I received an impartation of faith at that time from the Word of God that would sustain me through the trials that were yet to come in my life.

When I later returned to Toronto, my brother Larry asked me how I kept my sanity through my ordeal. I simply told him that I read the Bible, specifically the Book of Matthew. His reply was, "Oh well, if that was the crutch that you needed, I guess it was good for you." I didn't argue. I just told my brother that he should read the Bible for himself and left it at that.

Hebrews 4:12 *For the word of God is living and powerful, and sharper than any two-edged sword, piercing even to the division of soul and spirit, and of joints and marrow, and is a discerner of the thoughts and intents of the heart.*

I Could Use Some Good News!

CHAPTER 10

"Don't You Touch That Phone!"

R suddenly showed up at our townhouse one day and told me that he wanted to leave the other woman and come back to me. He said, however, that he would have to fly back to Winnipeg to get his things. Our baby boy was sick with pneumonia at the time, so he suggested he take our daughter with him to make it easier for me to visit Carl in the hospital. That way, I could spend more time with him without having to worry about getting babysitters for Josie.

I know it is hard to believe, but I trusted him again. I wanted so much to believe that he was telling me the truth. I'm not sure that I even knew what it meant to be in love with a man but I do know that to me, marriage was a serious commitment, and I was willing to do anything I had to do to make it work. One week went by, then two, then three. During that time when I stayed for many hours each day with Carl in the hospital, I would sometimes be allowed to take him out of his oxygen tent and carry him up and down the hallways. My heart was torn in little pieces as he would reach out with his chubby little arms to any man that looked to him like his father and cry, "Papa, Papa."

For the first few weeks that Josie was in Winnipeg with her father, I would phone every night and speak to her, but gradually, they (my husband and the woman he was with) would make excuses about why they could not bring her to the phone, that she was sleeping or she was being bathed, etc. It was then that I remembered the words that R had said to me when he brought Josie home from Italy, "*I should have left her there with my parents!*" I was horrified at the time that he would even have thought such a thing but then I felt perhaps I was overreacting and I had put it out of my mind.

Chapter 10

One of my neighbors was a Baptist Christian and she had invited me to a Bible study with her pastor, Hans. I told her of my fears that my husband had lied to me again and my concern that he was not going to bring my daughter back. She contacted her pastor and I am so thankful for those compassionate Christians who came to my aid in my time of need. Hans and May helped me arrange to have a garage sale of the few items I owned, so I could raise money to fly to Winnipeg to bring Josie back. We decided that it would be best for me to vacate my apartment and this kind and generous couple who had three small children of their own told me to come and live with them until I was ready to return to Toronto.

I had just brought Carl home from the hospital, so the two of us moved in with the pastor and his wife. I was sitting on the sofa talking with May when I noticed that little Carl was sitting glassy eyed on the chair in the corner of the living room. I asked May for a thermometer and, after discovering he had a very high temperature, we immediately rushed him back to the hospital where he would need to remain until the fever came down. May told me not to worry, that she would bring Carl home while I was travelling to Winnipeg to bring my daughter back.

I contacted the police in Winnipeg and told them of my plight so they agreed to meet me at the airport and accompany me to pick up my daughter. Hans and May gave me the phone number of another pastor and his wife in Winnipeg that I could contact if anything went wrong. I didn't think it would be necessary but they persuaded me to take the number with me anyway. Hans and May called and told them about my situation and that I might need their help.

This was to be the first time I was to fly. It was in the middle of winter with deep, clean white snow sitting in thick chunks on fence posts and hanging over the edge of the rooftops on the rows of wooden houses lining the streets as we drove. I gazed intently out of the car window as I silently cried out in my heart, *Please God, keep my babies safe and help me to bring Josie home.*

I don't remember boarding the plane. I just remember arriving at the airport in Winnipeg where a very tall police officer met me. I felt as small as an insect as I looked up at him. He took me to the station where I proceeded to relate my story again. The officers asked me to show them my custody papers. "What do you mean?" I asked.

"You're legally separated aren't you?" replied one of the officers.

"Well, I don't know what you mean by legally," I said. "My husband just left me and took my daughter away to live with him and another woman."

"We're sorry, lady, but if you are still married, there's nothing we can do to help you." I sat there in a daze. I couldn't believe my ears. I was 27 years old, and knew nothing at all about divorce or custody or any such matters. All I knew was that my baby girl had been snatched away from me and my broken heart was bleeding as I was calmly and cold heartedly being informed that there was nothing that could be done to help me.

I remembered the piece of paper with my contact's name and asked if I could use the phone. My fingers were trembling as I dialed the number in front of me. Much to my relief, the couple was at home and they told me to wait at the station as they would come immediately to pick me up. We drove to a public phone booth (we didn't have cell phones in 1972) and I called R. His girlfriend answered and said that he was at work. I didn't let her know that I was in Winnipeg. As far as she knew, I was calling from Sault Ste. Marie. I honestly do not remember if I asked her then what their address was in case I would like to mail something to my daughter or if I had known it before. All I know is, we drove quickly to their home and rang the doorbell.

What a surprised look was on her face when she opened the door and saw me standing there. She immediately said she had better call R at work. A mother's fury rose up in me at that moment and I exclaimed while pointing my finger at her, "Don't you

Chapter 10

touch that phone!" Josie came running into the room, and as the young woman lifted her into her arms, I shouted, "Give me my baby!"

She said, "But her snowsuit is in the washing machine." Now, my daughter had not seen me for over six weeks and my angry tone frightened her so she started to cry and cling to the young woman who happened to be very pregnant.

I stood transfixed until the pastor's wife said, "Just go and take her in your arms and she will remember you."

I did just that and my Josie wrapped her little arms around my neck and cried, "Mommy, Mommy, Mommy." I removed my red, woolen winter coat and wrapped it around her as we raced back to the airport where I boarded the next flight to Sault Ste. Marie. It was a miracle that the plane was ready at just that moment to take off. It is still amazing to me how everything fell into place like clockwork.

We continued to live with Pastor Hans and May in Sault Ste. Marie until I called my sister and told her everything that had happened. I then boarded a bus with my children, making the eight or so hour journey to Toronto. While I did not know how we were going to manage, I knew that somehow we would.

Once again, my sister was there for me when I needed her. My parents were both in poor health and living in a small apartment, so it was impossible for us to stay with them. At the time, Gil was house sitting what was actually an upstairs apartment. We lived with her until the downstairs neighbor complained about the pitter patter of little feet overhead. While we waited for acceptance of yet another application to Ontario Housing, my sister found a friend for us to live with in an area of Toronto known as "The Beaches".

Unfortunately, my daughter had a traumatic experience while we stayed with this couple and their four year old son. Little Carl had become ill with a fever and I had to take him to the doctor while I left Josie with this lady whom I will call "A". It was in the middle of winter and I had to travel by streetcar, so it took us quite a while. Stopping at the pharmacy on the way home to fill a prescription for Carl, I gave the information to the pharmacist and he said in a loud voice in front of a crowded store, "We don't fill prescriptions here for people on welfare." I was not only humiliated but desperate to obtain medicine for my child. I had to go to another pharmacy!

When I finally arrived home, I heard my daughter screaming hysterically, "Mommy, Mommy."

I asked A," Where is Josie?"

She replied, "She has been bad."

I yelled, "Where is she??!!" I ran upstairs and followed her voice until I found her locked in a dark closet. She was terrified and I was astonished and horrified that "A" could be so cruel to my little girl who was not even three years old. We had to find a way to leave immediately.

Gil arranged for us to stay with her friend Don's family who was Catholic. Hughie and Ann already had twelve children of their own, but they still found room in their hearts to take us in. They also lived in "The Beaches" area. My brother Stan purchased a blue baby stroller for me, which was a great help. I hadn't had one, up to that point, and used to carry my babies everywhere in my arms. Now Carl could sit in the stroller while Josie sat on the handle bar with my arms around her and off we would go.

We were very close to the beach, south of Queen Street where there was a park to play in, and I still love that neighborhood. Today, my daughter and her husband and children live in "The Beaches," and I believe they even go to the same park. I truly appreciated that family for helping us. They had a little room on the third floor where my children and I could sleep and when my son woke up for a bottle in the night I would have to carry him down three flights of stairs to the kitchen while trying to keep him quiet so as not to wake up the rest of the family.

The day finally arrived when an apartment was available for us in a new government housing building in Scarborough, a suburb of Toronto, east of the city. It had two bedrooms and was

Chapter 10

just perfect. My sister once again came to our rescue and, with the help of a couple of her friends, supplied us with the basic furniture that we needed. There was plenty of space in the large, scantily furnished rooms for the children to run around and play. Quite a number of single parent families lived in the building and the women got together and started a small day care in one of the recreation rooms. We would take turns caring for the children so that each mother had at least one or two mornings a week to do errands while their babies would be looked after. Later, I found employment with a temporary agency working at part time office assignments as I was allowed a certain amount of income over my government allowance. A couple of the ladies who helped run our little daycare offered to babysit for me during my assignments.

R was pressuring me to give him a divorce. I called him often to see if he would change his mind until one day, I received a call from his girlfriend who pleaded with me to stop calling him because every time he got off the phone with me, he physically abused her. So, I reluctantly faced reality and went to a Legal Aide lawyer provided to me because I was on welfare assistance. That was the reason R had wanted me to go through with the proceedings rather than him so that he would not have to pay a lawyer himself.

The attorney was a soft spoken and gentle man. Even so, I was overcome with nervousness as I sat across from him behind a huge, highly polished, dark, wooden desk with a glass top. I think I had two appointments to discuss details and then it was time to go to court. I was relieved when my brother Stan insisted on coming with me. I felt so small, helpless and insignificant as we entered that large, cold court room. Feelings of failure and rejection invaded my being as I looked at R sitting with a beautiful young woman with long blonde hair. The proceedings did not take long. I had a female judge and she was appalled at the circumstances that I and my children had been left in, so she granted me full custody not even giving visiting rights to my now former spouse.

Just like that, my life, and Josie and Carl's lives are irreversibly altered, I thought.

"How do you feel Ronnie?"

"Gee, Stan, I don't know. I guess I don't really feel anything. I don't feel glad, if that's what you mean. Thank you so much for being here with me. I don't think I could have done this by myself."

"Let's get out of here and have something to eat before I take you home, okay?"

"Well, I *am* kind of hungry now. I haven't eaten since yesterday; I was so nervous."

Later at home, Josie peered through a window out of our apartment in Scarborough. "Look, Papa's coming, Papa's coming!"

How can I tell her that her daddy is gone and never coming back? She's only two and one-half years old! Oh God, my heart is breaking for her. How am I going to comfort her? Carl was only one and one-half years old and even he remembered his papa. *How did my life come to this?* I thought.

Even though R had left me penniless in Sault Ste. Marie, I had kept hoping that somehow he would come to his senses. Now, I felt the full impact of the daunting responsibility of raising my children on my own. Fearful thoughts invaded my mind asking me, *Whatever will become of your children if you die?* I became obsessed with this thought. There came a point in time that I was even afraid to cross the street in case I would be hit by a car and my children would have no mother—no one to look after them. My heart's cry was, *OH GOD, PLEASE LET ME LIVE!* I begged Him to allow me to live long enough for Josie and Carl to become adults and able to take care of themselves. Somehow, I knew He would.

Chapter 10

Psalm 146:7-10
Who executes justice for the oppressed,
Who gives food to the hungry.
The LORD gives freedom to the prisoners.
The LORD opens the eyes of the blind;
The LORD raises those who are bowed down;
The LORD loves the righteous.
The LORD watches over the strangers;
He relieves the fatherless and widow;
But the way of the wicked
He turns upside down.
The LORD shall reign forever—Your God,
O Zion, to all generations. Praise the LORD!

CHAPTER 11

"Please, God, Just Get Us Through The Night!"

When Josie was about three and one-half years old, she became very ill with tonsillitis and needed surgery to have her tonsils removed. What was supposed to have been a simple tonsillectomy soon became a matter of life and death for my little girl. She had come in contact with chicken pox in our apartment building and developed a very high fever after the operation. At the same time, my dear mother was calling me almost every day, asking me to bring her grandchildren to see her. I was afraid to tell her how desperately ill Josie was, so I just kept making excuses and promising to come to visit soon.

More than being afraid to tell my mother that her granddaughter was in the hospital, I absolutely did not want her to find out that I had let the children's father take Carl back to Winnipeg for a week. Yes, I know what you are thinking. *What!? How could you agree to something like that after what you went through with Josie?* I had felt that it was only right to tell R about his daughter being deathly ill, so he came with his wife to see her. They offered to take Carl so I could spend all my time at the hospital with Josie. I was overwhelmed and exhausted. At the same time, I was glad for Carl that R was taking an interest in his little son. I am happy to say that they did bring Carl back as promised and that the Lord answered my prayers for Josie. I was finally able to take her home. As soon as my daughter was well enough, I had planned to take the children to visit their grandmother. Regrettably, I was not to have that opportunity.

Soon after Josie's recovery, Mummy died. She told our father one night that she had terrible heartburn and went to sleep on the sofa so as not to disturb him. Daddy went into shock after he

Chapter 11

discovered her in the morning. She had died of a massive heart attack in her sleep even though her doctor had just told her earlier that month, "You'll never die of a heart attack. You're as strong as an ox." That was April 1, 1975.

Gil called me to come to our parents' apartment. As the family gathered around our dad, my sister noticed that he looked very strange. It was a good thing that she was so alert because he was experiencing several mild strokes as he sat there. An ambulance was called and he was rushed to the hospital where he remained during his wife's funeral. Our Aunt Bertha stayed with him while we were all at the burial.

After my mother passed away, I would visit Daddy at his apartment on Spadina Avenue. He was nervous about me bringing the children inside because of all the medications he had to take. He had had several strokes by that time and was in very poor health. He was afraid that Josie or Carl might find their way into the medicine cabinet and harm themselves. So, we usually met him in the little park across the street or at the playground.

One time, I found him sitting on a park bench and he said, "I like to sit outside as much as I can because I don't know how much longer I will be able to enjoy the sound of the birds chirping and the leaves rustling in the wind." In my heart, I knew he would not be around much longer. He told me that he used to meet a friend at the park who was a Holocaust survivor who had shown him the number on his arm.

I had recently read *The Prophet* by Kahlil Gibran and thought that Daddy might enjoy it, too. When I presented it to him, he surprised me by saying, "I've read it already and others like it. I'm not interested. They don't have any answers for me."

When my father was in Mount Sinai Hospital after one of his strokes, I managed to sneak my daughter in with me. Josie was tall for four years old and children under six were not allowed to visit. I said she was six and the three of us enjoyed our little victory.

Daddy spent the final months of his life in a hospital on Bloor Street in Toronto where I was allowed to bring both his grandchildren to see him.

One thing my father said to me on one of those visits was, "I want you to know that I have always loved your mother."

My last visit is etched in my memory forever. When I went to look for him in his room he was lying on his bed looking as white as the sheet that covered him. I aroused him and we went to the cafeteria together. He kept telling me that they were not giving him the correct medication. I spoke to the nurse, but she said that everything was okay. They told me that he was mentally unstable and did not understand what was best for him.

Looking back, if I had the knowledge and confidence I do now, I would have been more aggressive, insisting that I speak with a doctor who would be able to give me more detailed information. Dad and I sat in the courtyard for a while with the children until he said that he was tired and needed to rest. As the elevator doors were closing when I said goodbye, I saw him standing in the hallway looking at me and somehow I knew that this was the last time I would see him alive.

A few days after that visit, I awoke one morning with a strong sense that I should call my father to see how he was doing. As I was preparing to drop my children off at the babysitter's and go to my part-time typist job, I noticed my broken eye glasses on a chair. My young son had accidentally sat on them but I could not be angry with him since I should not have left them on a chair in the first place and he was, after all, only three years old.

So now, I had to try to get my glasses fixed along with everything else on my agenda. I pushed back the thought of calling my dad, deciding to do it as soon as I got home from work. I could hardly concentrate that day as the gnawing feeling to call the hospital would not leave me. During my morning break I went to another floor in the building to pick up a cup of coffee. As I was waiting for the elevator, the paper cup suddenly fell from my hand

Chapter 11

onto the floor. I was not feeling dizzy and I knew that I had not loosened my grip on the cup. I thought it very strange but did not make any more of it at the time.

During my lunch break I went to the optometrist to see about fixing my glasses. By the time I finished work, picked up my children, cooked dinner and tended to everything that needed to be done, I was exhausted and went to bed early with my babies without calling my father.

That night I dreamed that I was with my father at the hospital while he was dying. I saw the doctors in white coats and watched them attempt to revive him. Somehow, I could hear what he was crying out in his heart to them. *Please let me go to be with Esther. I just want to be with Esther!* But no one could hear him. I felt the anguish of his emotions as he tried to make himself understood. Then there was silence. I awoke to hear the phone ringing and I immediately knew that my father had died. (It was August 27, 1975.) I got out of bed and answered the phone. "Daddy just died," Gilda told me.

"I know," I replied in a calm voice. Later, at the funeral when I didn't show any emotion, my family thought there might be something wrong with me. I didn't understand it at the time, but I believe the Lord gave me peace about my father's death.

I later found out from the hospital that the time that he went into a coma was the same time that my cup of coffee fell from my hand to the floor that day. God, in His great mercy, had allowed me the privilege of knowing what was in my father's heart during his final moments on this earth. The full meaning of this experience was not to be revealed to me until 1982 in Johannesburg, South Africa.

Later that year, a social worker came to meet with the single mothers of our building and told us that we were eligible to apply for a government grant to take a course at the local community college. I jumped at the opportunity and received a student loan for a two year program. This particular college had a day care that was run by the psychology students so I was able to take my children to school with me. I chose a course in psychology because I thought this might open the door for me to help those who were suffering with emotional and mental problems. I was doing quite well until the time came for the students to take part in clinical internships.

We were taken to a mental institution in Toronto. As we entered the dark, red brick building, we were ushered through a dimly lit hallway. My legs began to tremble and I felt weak. *I don't know if I can do this*, I thought. *I don't have a good feeling about this at all. It is so gloomy and depressing in here.* Thoughts of my mother's unthinkable experience came flooding into my mind. Then it happened. I was told what my assignment would be. I was to assist the doctors in administering electric shock treatments! I was appalled at the idea and began to feel a desperate need to flee from that place as fast as I could. I didn't hear a thing after that while the doctors explained to us what our work would consist of. I kept my calm and was greatly relieved when we were able to depart.

After we returned to the school, I spoke to my counselor and told him that I was withdrawing from the course. I couldn't bring myself to tell him about my mother. It was a dark family secret that I kept hidden. Instead, I told him that I had experienced too much stress with both my parents passing away that year before I started college. He tried to convince me to reconsider, but my mind was made up. I wanted no part of what I considered to be inhumane treatment of vulnerable patients.

It was while babysitting for some of the ladies in my apartment building that I met Marilyn. We became friends and she invited me to come to her Baptist church. She also told me about Katherine Kuhlman who had a weekly television program during the 1970's. I watched one episode and really did not understand any of it except that I was struck by Miss Kuhlman's flamboyant appearance.

Chapter 11

My experience at Marilyn's Baptist Church was another one of those *I hope no one can tell that I am Jewish* moments. I had received the unconditional love of God through the two Baptist ministers and their wives during my time of great need in Sault Ste. Marie. Unfortunately, this encounter was to be much different. Anyway, I agreed to go to this church which was within walking distance from my apartment. I took my son and daughter with me and the Sunday school workers ushered them to the children's area downstairs.

The church was packed and my friend was not there that day. I was seated somewhere in the middle and enjoyed the singing somewhat, not really knowing what to expect or what to do as I did not have any church experience at all. When the minister began to speak, I couldn't believe what I was hearing. He was talking about all the divorce and financial problems taking place in Canada and that it was entirely the fault of the Jews. "If Canada had not let the Jews in after the war, we would not be going through this," he said.

I was already anxious just attending a church service. Now, as I tried to stay calm, it felt like high school all over again. I was hoping that my face which felt like it was on fire was not beet red, as I always blushed when I was nervous. I wanted to run out of there as fast as I could but felt it would show everyone I was a Jew. I wondered, *How can I grab my children out of Sunday school without making a scene?* So, I endured until the end of the meeting when there was an alter call and one person went to the front for prayer. Of course, I didn't understand anything that was going on. I was just thankful that we were finally dismissed.

I quickly exited the sanctuary, retrieving my children before anyone had a chance to engage me in a conversation. Josie and Carl seemed to have had a fun time so I was glad about that.

Isn't it interesting how the enemy of our soul will use anyone he can to prevent us from coming to know our Messiah? My enemy was not that Baptist minister. *For we do not wrestle against flesh and blood, but against principalities, against powers, against the rulers of the darkness of this age, against spiritual hosts of wickedness in the heavenly places* (Ephesians 6:12). I never spoke to my friend about what happened. I just told her that I was not interested in going back to her church.

Sometime later I met "S" at one of those singles get-togethers that a girlfriend had convinced me to attend. He told me he was divorced but a few years later, I was not so sure that he had been truthful with me. He took us on a vacation one summer through Mexico to Central America where we stayed a few weeks in a small dwelling one of his friends owned in Costa Rica.

Driving through Mexico and Central America was a most memorable experience. There were stark contrasts of wealth and poverty; poverty such as I had never seen before. Traveling during the rainy season, one could see families living in makeshift shacks that were constructed out of anything and everything; sheets of aluminum, cardboard, sticks, and boards. Outside wood fires or stone ovens were common and the people moved about in the mud, cooking their meals and sweeping their huts while using colorful handkerchiefs to swish at the constant swarms of tiny flies. I still remember one beautiful young girl who came alongside our Volkswagen camper with a tray of bread on her head to sell to us. At that point, everything that I had been through seemed as nothing compared to what I was witnessing.

When we traveled through Nicaragua, we had no idea that a revolution was just beginning. It was late afternoon and we were attempting to get to the town just below the winding mountain road we were on in order to sleep for the night. I am still in awe of how God protected us. Suddenly, out of a clear blue sky, huge storm clouds rolled in, and the sky became as dark as midnight while the rain came pouring down in torrents. It was so strong and fierce that we had to park our camper in a small clearing by the side of the road to wait it out. It was impossible to drive any further. The rain and thunder continued all night as I lay awake,

Chapter 11

praying to God to protect us. I started asking Him to forgive me for just about everything I could think of, if only He would allow me and my children to come through this night safely. "Please, God, just get us through the night!"

The day finally dawned with the sun rising and the blue sky appearing. As we resumed our journey, we were amazed to see how close we actually were to the bottom of the mountain and the entrance to the town. The alarming sight that awaited us was indescribable. Black flags were mounted everywhere. Distraught mourners were wailing while bodies were strewn about to and fro. I had never seen anything like this in my life. I was dumbfounded. We managed to find someone who could speak a little English, and he told us that a revolution had begun. There had been fighting and had we come through the night before we surely would have been shot. Oh the awesome mercy of our Lord! It was at that moment that I realized that the storm the night before was not a coincidence. God Himself had created it to keep us from going into the village below.

Romans 5:8 *But God demonstrates His own love toward us, in that while we were still sinners, Christ died for us.*
Psalm 29:3 *The voice of the Lord is over the waters; the God of Glory thunders; the Lord is over many waters.*

Costa Rica is one of the most picturesque places I have ever traversed. It was the only democracy in the region at that time. I found the city of San Jose to be a bustling, crowded place with dusty streets. My nostrils were invaded with various fragrances from spices to meats cooking in ovens in the open air restaurants to vegetables in the marketplace. The streets were teaming with the most friendly and hospitable people. A short drive from the city took us up into lush, rich mountain farmland. Here, we would be greeted on the roadside with the broad welcoming smiles of the indigenous people. Their colorful clothing reflected the magnificent majesty of the landscape. One moment we would be in a tropical jungle-like area with gigantic, emerald-green ferns and forests that blocked out the sun. A short drive later we would be travelling high into the mountains with the rain visibly falling from a cloud on the horizon.

Brilliant hues of every color of the rainbow burst upon my senses. Costa Rica was imprinted in my memory forever. It was as if we were moving through a most beautifully created canvas of lush landscapes

It was amusing to ask for directions in San Jose. For example, we were looking for the post office and were advised, "Go 10 meters north, 5 meters west, and you will be there." So, there we were, gazing down at the pavement measuring our footsteps! Also, we purchased a map, followed a road on it, and found that it led us nowhere. When we finally found a tourist center, they told us, "Oh, do not follow the roads on the map. Many of those roads have not been built yet!" Next door to where we were living, in a friend's humble dwelling (which had only cold water for the shower), was a fruit farm. The owners used to regularly supply us with freshly squeezed nectar from various tropical fruits. Costa Rica was truly, to us, an oasis in the midst of a dry and thirsty land.

Psalm 19:1-4 *The heavens declare the glory of God; And the firmament shows His handiwork. Day unto day utters speech, And night unto night reveals knowledge. There is no speech nor language where their voice is not heard. Their line has gone out through all the earth, And their words to the end of the world.*

CHAPTER 12

"There Has To Be A Change In My Life!"

This latest man in my life, "S", had family in Africa Don't even ask me why I agreed to take my children to Africa with him. I have struggled with this question myself. I only know that I had desperately wanted to escape my past, and that I was looking for security and safety in all the wrong places.

It was 1981, six years after my parents died, that we relocated to Zimbabwe (formally Rhodesia). We first stayed in a hotel in Harare while we searched for rental housing. If I remember correctly, it was winter during the month of July. The afternoons were sunny and warm, while the early mornings and nights were very cold. There was no central heating but we had a small space heater, supplied to us, in our room. Early in the morning, I would turn on the heater and lay the children's clothes on the floor in front of it to warm them before Josie and Carl would get dressed. We ate our meals in the hotel dining room. I don't remember meeting many other people, if any, while staying at this hotel. I do remember that the children and I thought it to be quite hilarious that we were given forks with which to eat our dishes of jello pudding. We were later told that the staff had stolen all the spoons! The African people we met there were very friendly and accommodating.

We found a house to rent in the suburbs of Harare where we lived for one year. While there, I sent my children to a British boarding school. S was not a man of great financial means. He had told me that he just had a sense of adventure and loved to travel. Later, when I found out more about him from his relatives, I wasn't so sure that his only reason for traveling was for adventure. I suspected he may have been on the run from place to place because of dishonesty in his business dealings. Of course, I didn't know any of that at the time.

Chapter 12

In Zimbabwe, he ran his own business of repairing cameras, while I found employment at a flower shop in town. I sometimes rode a bus to work and, except for one other British woman, I was the only white person on the bus. The others were mostly African women with babies wrapped on their backs with a cloth that tied in the front. I was always concerned that the babies' heads might get crushed on the back of the seats as the rickety bus travelled over bumpy roads. However, these women seemed to be very skilled and experienced at this and their babies appeared quite content as they slept snuggled on their mothers' backs.

Being new in the country, I did not know anyone that I felt comfortable with to babysit my children while I was at work. I was told that the British boarding schools supplied the best education in Zimbabwe. As heart wrenching as it was for me, I made the decision to send my children to boarding school. I felt it would be the safest place for them to be until I could figure out what else to do. I can't even imagine how difficult this must have been for Josie and Carl who were now nine and ten years old.

One thing they had to re-learn at boarding school was how to hold a fork. Josie and Carl were told not to "shovel" their food. We, in North America hold the fork like a spoon. The British hold it "upside down" and push their food onto it with a knife. Boarding school was a normal and accepted part of the British culture, but there was nothing normal about it for me. I actually wrote letters to my children every day. I would simply tell them about my activities each day and, of course, that I loved them and missed them. I brought them home on weekends until the matrons told me that by taking them away from the school every weekend they were not able to establish friendships with the other children. I found out much later, after we had left Zimbabwe, that the matrons would not allow Josie and Carl to answer my letters.

Meanwhile, I knew that I could not go on living a lie in front of my children. I was not married to S and it troubled me greatly. I also couldn't believe that I had been so reckless and irresponsible with the lives of my children. I was feeling desperate to take Josie and Carl away from this man who was becoming more and more controlling towards me. Dreadful thoughts were bombarding my mind such as, *Just look at the mess you have made of your life now and not only your life but the lives of your children! You're a complete failure!* "Oh God," I cried out one night, "there has to be a change in my life or I just know I am going to die! I feel like I am standing on the edge of a cliff."

The very next morning, at the flower shop where I was employed as a bookkeeper, I had a prophetic encounter with a woman named Jenny. I had been working there for a while and had managed to mess up the books pretty badly. This was another one of my attempts to bluff my way into an employment position that I was not fully qualified for. It backfired on me this time as there was no one to turn to for instruction. I had lied about being a bookkeeper and now it was time to face the music. Amazingly, I was not fired. The owner asked an accountant to come in and straighten out the books so I would have an opportunity to try again. I was so undeserving of the grace that was shown to me!

Jenny was a born-again Christian and perhaps, unbeknownst to me, my boss was one too. She brought her two young daughters and three-year-old son with her. I watched her three blond, blue eyed, angelic-looking children play on the grass outside the office window. Jenny said to me, "Do you see that little boy? He is a miracle from God." She then proceeded to tell me her story. "I had another son and when he was two years old, he drowned in our swimming pool. I couldn't get over my grief. I was not even able to care for my two girls as I went into a deep depression. I went to my Catholic priest for help but he couldn't say anything to ease my sorrow and guilt. Then, one day a friend of mine took me to see her Christian minister. He spoke and prayed with me for a long while. As I was driving home, I saw Jesus standing in front of me. I had to stop my car and pull over to the side of the road. Jesus comforted me and took away my guilt and shame. I re-

Chapter 12

ceived His forgiveness of my sins and asked Him to come into my heart. He also told me that God would give me another son and that child you see out there is him." Jenny then asked me to go to a Christian movie with her about Joni, the girl who had dived into a swimming pool and hit her head and became paralyzed from the neck down.

As Jenny was relating her story to me I was thinking, *Poor woman, she has been through so much. If she wants to think that she saw Jesus, who am I to take that away from her? If that is what she needs to keep her from falling apart, I'm not going to say anything.*

So, when she invited me to the movie, I declined her offer. She looked me square in the eyes and declared with authority, "Can't you see that you are standing on the edge of a cliff and I am trying to keep you from falling off!"

This statement shocked me as those were the very words that I had cried out to God the night before! I was so frightened by the accuracy of Jenny's statement that I replied in an angry tone, "Jenny, don't you ever talk to me like that again! What you believe is good for you but leave me alone!"

The Lord Himself was speaking through Jenny. We seldom know how powerful our words can be. I know that Jenny was not aware of what I had prayed the night before but she was obedient to speak what the Holy Spirit was telling her to say to me. She was not moved by my angry response. She became a very special friend to me right up until the time that we left Zimbabwe and, God knows, I needed a friend. Jenny was not shocked or deterred by my rejection because she knew that God does not look at the outward appearance as man does, but He looks at the heart (1 Samuel 16:7).

Not long after that, the political climate in Zimbabwe began turning more and more ominous with Robert Mugabe as President. So we left Zimbabwe and her magnificent jacaranda blossoms to live in South Africa. The last time Jenny and I were together, she was driving me to the boarding school to take a birthday cake there for my children. Since their birthdays were just one day apart, they only needed one cake to share with the other students. I told her that we were leaving soon and I asked her, "Jenny, you have children. Why aren't you and your husband leaving?"

I have never forgotten what she immediately replied. "God has told the Christians to stay, and we are staying!"

Driving from Zimbabwe to South Africa was a great education in God's creation for the children and me. We saw huge baobab trees and gigantic ant hills along the road.

We finally arrived in Johannesburg which was a large, dusty, bustling city. It was so dusty because it was during a time of drought. The grass was scorched and yellow and, until I became acclimatized to the high altitude, I felt dizzy much of the time. We stayed with S's cousin until we found our own apartment. Auntie Stella embraced us, smothering us with hugs and kisses as she was so happy to see us again. She had come to visit us in Canada some months before we travelled to Africa and she had assured us that there were no lions prowling on the streets of Johannesburg!

Stella was kind, generous, and matronly with a delightful personality. The children took to her immediately. We also met Auntie Lizzie who was a little more serious but very loving. It was during our stay in South Africa that I began hearing stories from S's family and I realized that he had not told me the whole truth about himself.

Auntie Stella lived in an older part of the city and did not have an indoor toilet. She did have a proper one with plumbing but it was in a concrete structure in the yard. Also, the electrical wiring in her house needed repair. It was not properly grounded. I was warned about being careful when using the washer/spin dryer while doing my laundry. I was to remember to pull the plug out of the socket before reaching into the water to retrieve the clothes from the washing machine unit to dump them into the spin dryer.

One day, I forgot to pull the plug! I was merrily doing my laundry, standing barefoot on a wet floor when I reached into el-

Chapter 12

bow deep water to pull out the clothes. I felt an electric shock run across my chest from the right side to the left and as I attempted to pull my arms out of the water, nothing happened! I couldn't move! I cried out, "Oh God," and suddenly my arms shot up out of the water over my head and I was free. I felt myself to see if I was still alive and amazingly, I was still breathing!

> Psalm 91:11-12 *For He shall give His angels charge over you, To keep you in all your ways. In their hands they shall bear you up, Lest you dash your foot against a stone.*

When I related this incident to S who was an electrician, he declared that I must be mistaken. He said that I could not possibly have lived through something like that considering all the physical circumstances, and at the very least, my hair would have turned white!

One Sunday morning we visited another relative living in one of the colored townships surrounding Johannesburg. We arrived at their home just when the family was returning from church. This mother of three lovely children asked me, "Are you taking your children to church?"

"No."

She immediately said, "How then are you going to teach them the fear and admonition of the Lord?!" That sentence reverberated in my conscience and it was not too long afterwards that Josie and Carl and I went together to church in Johannesburg.

Another significant event that took place shortly before we went to church in South Africa was that I went to see one of the Damian movies that was playing at the time. I was impacted by the ending where evil triumphed over good and I could not reconcile it in my mind. I just knew that ultimately, good has to triumph over evil.

There Has To Be A Change

> Matthew 28:1-10 *Now after the Sabbath, as the first day of the week began to dawn, Mary Magdalene and the other Mary came to see the tomb. And behold, there was a great earthquake; for an angel of the Lord descended from heaven, and came and rolled back the stone from the door, and sat on it. His countenance was like lightning, and His clothing as white as snow. And the guards shook for fear of him, and became like dead men.*
>
> *But the angel answered and said to the women, "Do not be afraid, for I know that you seek Jesus who was crucified. He is not here; for He is risen, as He said. Come see the place where the Lord lay. And go quickly and tell His disciples that He is risen from the dead, and indeed He is going before you into Galilee; there you will see Him. Behold, I have told you."*
>
> *So they went out quickly from the tomb with fear and great joy, and ran to bring His disciples word.*
>
> *And as they went to tell His disciples, behold, Jesus met them, saying, "Rejoice!" So they came and held Him by the feet and worshipped Him. Then Jesus said to them 'Do not be afraid. Go and tell My brethren to go to Galilee, and there they will see Me.*

So, here I was three months after leaving Zimbabwe entering a church auditorium full of hundreds of people. To me, their voices were like the whooshing in a forest of majestic white pine trees swaying in the wind. I walked as if in slow motion to the front, close to the platform.

Gwynn, a Christian man, had brought me to church. Only a few weeks before that, I had met him at a luncheon at the home of a Canadian woman I met through S. Only God could have orchestrated the circumstances that day. Gwynn had been invited at the last minute only because the hostess, a Canadian woman married to a South African, had unexpectedly come across him on the street while he was shopping in downtown Johannesburg. She used to attend Rhema Bible Church but had not been there for about three years. When he met me at the luncheon, he told me about his church and said that I was welcome to bring my children to visit it. I replied that I didn't know if I would be interested. Gwynn handed me a piece of paper with his phone number

Chapter 12

in case I changed my mind and I quickly put it in my pocket. I didn't want S to see it because I was pretty sure that he would try to prevent me from taking my children to church.

I felt compelled to call Gwynn one morning from work and we met in the park for lunch. I believe he had been praying for me. He asked me what I thought about the story of Adam and Eve and I replied that I thought it was a fairy tale. Then, he said "Let's pray."

"Right here? Out loud?"

"Sure." So, he prayed and I must confess that I did not really understand what he was praying about. Later, he asked me, "What do you want most in your life at this moment, a car, a house, a husband?"

I immediately exclaimed, "I want the truth in my life!"

He shouted, "Praise the Lord!" He then asked me again if I would like to come to church on Sunday, and I asked him what kind of a church it was. He said, "A Christian church."

I exclaimed, "Oh, I can't come. They won't let me in. I'm Jewish." I honestly believed what I was saying because of my past experience with the Christian church.

He said, "We're all Jews. We, the Gentiles, are grafted in."

Romans 11:22-24 Therefore consider the goodness and severity of God: on those who fell, severity; but toward you, goodness, if you continue in His goodness. Otherwise you also will be cut off. And they also, if they do not continue in unbelief, will be grafted in, for God is able to graft them in again. For if you were cut out of the olive tree which is wild by nature, and were grafted contrary to nature into a cultivated olive tree, how much more will these, who are natural branches, be grafted into their own olive tree?

The Holy Spirit knew exactly what I needed to hear to set me free to say, "Yes, I'll come."

The next Sunday morning on July 18, 1982, my children and I met Gwynn at the bus stop in Hillbrow, where he picked us up and drove us to church. I had to meet him at the bus stop because I was afraid to tell S where we were going as I knew he would try to stop us. I made some excuse to go out with the children. I don't remember now what reason I gave to him. As we stood on the corner until Gwynn arrived, we were in the company of some Christians who were waiting for the bus to take them to Rhema Bible Church. I remember thinking how strange these people were. One young man, Danny, who the children and I were later privileged to become friends with, had a guitar and was leading the crowd in singing to pass the time. They all seemed so ridiculously happy!

After we arrived at the church, Gwynn escorted us from the parking lot to the lobby inside and gently suggested that I let one of the ushers take Josie and Carl upstairs to the Children's Ministry. I was a little reluctant to send them off without me, but Gwynn assured me that they would be well looked after. They seemed happy to go, so I agreed. As we entered the auditorium, I said, "I feel strange." I had never known such a sense of peace before. The anxiety that had plagued me since childhood seemed to vanish as I stood there in the midst of angelic sounds of worship to the King of Kings. I didn't realize that I was experiencing the tangible presence of the Lord.

The only thing I remember of Pastor Ray McCauley's sermon that morning was that he was preparing for a trip to the United States and this would be his last Sunday preaching until he returned. The message was a blur to my ears except for the altar call at the end. When he asked if anyone wanted to receive Jesus into their heart, my hand shot up like a bullet. But, when he asked all who raised their hands to come forward, I felt as if my feet were glued to the floor and my arms were heavy weights stuck to my sides. I was paralyzed with fear. Gwynn gently nudged me forward and said, "Go! Go and get your blessing." I went forward and prayed for the forgiveness of my sins and then we were ushered to a room with Christians waiting to pray with us.

Chapter 12

I was overwhelmed by the presence of God and the love and the forgiveness of Jesus. I had been on a long, dusty road all the years of my life in search of food and water and now I was alone with the one who is the Bread of Life, who gives living water freely to those who ask (John 4). The people around me faded and didn't matter. This was my moment of destiny with Jesus!

Psalm 42:1-2 *As the deer pants for the water brooks, so pants my soul for You, O God. My soul thirsts for God, for the living God. When shall I come and appear before God?*

At the same time that I was praying, Josie and Carl asked Jesus into their hearts in the Children's church. *But Jesus said, "Let the little children come to me; and do not forbid them for of such is the Kingdom of Heaven"* (Matthew 19:14).

I will never forget that day on July 18, 1982 when my lifetime search for the Truth had brought me to Rhema Bible Church where I was changed forever. Everything I had been longing for came together in one unforgettable explosion of light that permeated my heart, soul and mind in a matter of seconds. The Holy Spirit revealed to me that Jesus is my Jewish Messiah, the Son of the living God. It was the beginning of a pilgrimage on this earth as a new creation in the Messiah. I finally knew who I was—the spiritual and physical seed of Abraham. I discovered my true identity. I was no longer forsaken but had become the Bride of God in whom He delights (Isaiah 62:4). No matter what my circumstance in this life, I had found my peace and rest and purpose in Him.

Isaiah 1:18 *"Come now, and let us reason together," Says the LORD, "Though your sins are like scarlet, They shall be as white as snow; Though they are red like crimson, They shall be as wool."*

Matthew 16:13-17 *When Jesus came into the region of Caesarea Philippi, He asked His disciples, saying, "Who do men say that I, the*

There Has To Be A Change

Son of Man, am?" So they said, "Some say John the Baptist, some Elijah, and others Jeremiah or one of the prophets." He said to them, "But who do you say that I am?" Simon Peter answered and said, "You are the Christ, the Son of the living God." Jesus answered and said to him, "Blessed are you, Simon Bar-Jonah, for flesh and blood has not revealed this to you, but My Father who is in heaven."

⁓

Rhema had a bookstore and Gwynn purchased Bibles for us as we did not possess any. Now, the children and I could read God's Word for ourselves. Josie and Carl purchased two beautiful wooden wall plaques for me with their allowance money from that same bookstore several months later. They presented them to me on my birthday. Written on one is Psalm 118.24 *This is the day the Lord has made; We will rejoice and be glad in it.* The other displays Psalm 100:2 *Serve the Lord with gladness; Come before His presence with singing.* Those wall plaques have traveled with me all these years and I have them hanging on my kitchen wall today.

After service on our first day at church, the children and I were invited to have lunch with some Christians in their home. I am forever thankful for the caring brothers and sisters in that fellowship who nurtured us during those first critical months.

There were trials and challenges to come but now we knew that we were not alone and could lean on Jesus who promises never to leave us or forsake us.

⁓

Hebrews 13:5 *Let your conduct be without covetousness; be content with such things as you have. For He Himself has said, "I will never leave you nor forsake you."*

⁓

A passion burned in my heart to know Jesus more intimately and, like a dry sponge, I soaked up every drop of the life-giving Word of God! I witnessed miracles of healing in the meetings at Rhema and continued to experience the Presence of the Lord in a powerful way. During worship I would often find myself on the floor between the rows of chairs. I knew nothing about being

Chapter 12

"slain in the spirit" but I was encountering the manifest Presence and Glory of God.

John 1:14 And the Word became flesh and dwelt among us, and we beheld His glory, the glory as of the only begotten of the Father, full of grace and truth.

Fear had been replaced with love so overwhelmingly and indescribably pure that it was tangible. As I walked the busy streets of Johannesburg, I now had a compassionate affection for the people around me. They were no longer meaningless masses of people. I saw them as lost souls marching to an endless eternity without hope. I had a burning desire to share with them all that Jesus had done on the cross for me so that they too could know the fullness of His love and forgiveness.

Zechariah 9:9 Rejoice greatly, O daughter of Zion!
Shout, O daughter of Jerusalem!
Behold, your King is coming to you;
He is just and having salvation,
Lowly and riding on a donkey,
A colt, the foal of a donkey.

One Saturday night after I was born again in 1982, I said to the Lord, "Jesus, I know that you have forgiven me but I can NEVER forgive myself." I was referring to the abortion I had many years earlier.

The next morning at the church which was filled with about 500 people, the pastor, who had no idea who I was, suddenly stopped in the middle of his sermon, swung around, pointed directly at me, and exclaimed, "If God has forgiven you, who are YOU not to forgive yourself!"

I felt as if I had been struck by lightning. I realized that I had been putting myself above the Creator of the universe; that I was in fact shaking my fist at God in defiance even though it might have appeared a noble thing to say. I asked Jesus to help me forgive myself, and I was finally set free.

God even revealed to me that my baby was a boy and his name was Daniel and I will see him one day in Heaven! I was once again struck with awe at the mercy of God towards me. There truly is no pit so deep that our Heavenly Father cannot reach into it and pull us out. Jesus Himself went to the lowest depths of the earth for us and defeated death and everything that it embodies.

> Psalm 40:2 *He also brought me up out of a horrible pit,*
> *Out of the miry clay,*
> *And set my feet upon a rock,*
> *And established my steps.*

Luke 7:36-50 *Then one of the Pharisees asked Him to eat with him. And He went to the Pharisee's house, and sat down to eat. And behold, a woman in the city who was a sinner, when she knew that Jesus sat at the table in the Pharisee's house, brought an alabaster flask of fragrant oil, and stood at His feet behind Him weeping; and she began to wash His feet with her tears, and wiped them with the hair of her head; and she kissed His feet and anointed them with the fragrant oil. Now when the Pharisee who had invited Him saw this, he spoke to himself saying, "This man, if He were a prophet, would know who and what manner of woman this is who is touching Him, for she is a sinner."*

And Jesus answered and said to him, "Simon, I have something to say to you."

So he said, "Teacher, say it."

"There was a certain creditor who had two debtors. One owed five hundred denarii and the other fifty. And when they had nothing to which to repay, he freely forgave them both. Tell me, therefore, which one will love him more?"

Simon answered and said, "I suppose the one whom he forgave more."

And He said to him, "You have rightly judged." Then He turned to the woman and said to Simon, "Do you see this woman? I entered your house; You gave Me no water for My feet, but she has washed my feet with her tears and wiped them with the hair of her head. You gave Me no kiss, but this woman has not ceased to kiss My feet since the time

Chapter 12

I came in. You did not anoint My head with oil, but this woman has anointed My feet with fragrant oil. Therefore, I say to you, her sins, which are many, are forgiven, for she loved much. But to whom little is forgiven, the same loves little."

Then He said to her, "Your sins are forgiven."

And those who sat at the table with Him began to say to themselves, "Who is this who even forgives sins?" Then He said to the woman "Your faith has saved you. Go in peace."

So great is His mercy that even though I have not forgotten what I have done, the trauma and the shame have been taken away. This allows me to talk about it openly so that I may be a comfort to others, just as the Bible says: *[He] comforts us in all our tribulation, that we may be able to comfort those who are in any trouble, with the comfort with which we ourselves are comforted by God* (II Corinthians 1:4).

I felt as if I had come face to face with God! Afterwards, people in that church told me that my face was glowing! It reminds me of the Scripture in Exodus 34:29-35 that says the face of Moses shone when he came down from Mt. Sinai after meeting with God.

A short while after I received that revelation about forgiving myself, Pastor Ray exclaimed during a Sunday morning service "If any one of you had a glimpse of hell for as little as one second you would say that you wouldn't even want someone like Hitler to go there!" That was another "God" moment for me. Once again, I felt that God was speaking directly to me. I was not taken on a supernatural journey into hell as some others have experienced but that statement went straight to my heart like an arrow. The Holy Spirit revealed to me what the reality of living forever in eternal damnation would be like. From that moment on, I had a burning desire to rescue a deceived humanity from falling into the pit of darkness forever. I had a vision in my mind where I would see multitudes of people with their arms raised in a cry for help that would never come because it was too late (Luke 16:19-31).

The eyes of my understanding were opened to the reality that every single person will one day stand before God to account for his own actions. God is the judge. What is required of me is to be obedient to His word. When Peter asked Jesus how many times he had to forgive his brother who had sinned against him, Jesus told him up to seventy times seven. In this life, we will have opportunity daily to forgive others so we must live a lifestyle of forgiveness. I ask myself, *Has anyone nailed me to a cross? Have I suffered in comparison to what Jesus suffered for me?* If I hold on to an offense, I am harming myself, not the other person. I recently heard someone say "Refusing to forgive is like drinking poison and expecting the other person to die." If I choose to walk in unforgiveness, I limit the plans and purposes of God in my life by hindering the flow of His Spirit through me. That, to me, is too high a price to pay. I choose to forgive and in so doing, I am releasing others so that I may walk in freedom.

Mark 11:25-26 *And whenever you stand praying, if you have anything against anyone, forgive him, that your Father in heaven may also forgive you your trespasses. But if you do not forgive, neither will your Father in heaven forgive your trespasses.*

Following Messiah

CHAPTER 13

"Jesus Still Loves You"

As soon as I was born again I was longing to know what had happened to my parents after they died. One evening, I was praying and asking God to heal my feet because I had bunions. As I previously mentioned, my mother also had bunions and they were pretty bad by the time she was in her 60's. That night, I had a dream. I saw two beautiful, perfect feet in front of me. In my dream, I knew they were my mother's feet and I said, "Ma, your feet are perfect!"

I did not see her face or even her body, just her feet, but I recognized her voice as she replied, "Yes dear and yours are, too." When I awoke the next morning the first thing I did was to look at my feet and to my disappointment, they were no different. Then I realized that God had given me that dream, so I would know that my beloved mother was indeed with the Lord with no more suffering and no more pain, and I could look forward to seeing her again.

Revelation 21:2-4 *Then I, John, saw the holy city, New Jerusalem, coming down out of heaven from God, prepared as a bride adorned for her husband.*

And I heard a loud voice from heaven saying, "Behold, the tabernacle of God is with men, and He will dwell with them, and they shall be His people. God Himself will be with them and be their God. And God will wipe away every tear from their eyes; there shall be no more death, nor sorrow, nor crying. There shall be no more pain, for the former things have passed away."

Philippians 3:20-21 *For our citizenship is in heaven, from which we also eagerly wait for the Savior, the Lord Jesus Christ, who will transform our lowly body that it may be conformed to His glorious body, according to the working by which He is able even to subdue all things to Himself.*

Chapter 13

What a joy it was to know this. By faith I know that by Jesus' stripes my feet have already been healed. So I wait in expectation for the manifestation of a miraculous straightening of my feet! Yesterday, today, and tomorrow are now. God's time is not our time. *But beloved, do not forget this one thing, that with the Lord one day is as a thousand years, and a thousand years as one day* (II Peter 3:8).

After coming to the realization that my mother was with the Lord, the Holy Spirit brought to my remembrance the dream that I had when my father had died. In my dream, he had been crying out to let him go to be with Esther. From that, I believe he had made his peace with God. So, I have great comfort in knowing that my parents are in the Presence of the Lord.

Luke 23:42-43 *Then he said to Jesus, "Lord, remember me when You come into Your kingdom." And Jesus said to him, "Assuredly, I say to you, today you will be with Me in Paradise."* (This Scripture is referring to the two thieves hanging on the cross with Jesus. The one had a repentant heart and acknowledged Him as the Son of God; the other did not.)

In that day it shall be said to Jerusalem: "Do not fear;
Zion, let not your hands be weak.
The LORD your God in your midst,
The Mighty One, will save;
He will rejoice over you with gladness,
He will quiet you with His love,
He will rejoice over you with singing" (Zephaniah 3:16-17).

I felt as though Yeshua (Jesus) had taken a giant brush and painted a new picture on the canvas of my life. I wanted everyone to know about this Jesus who had set me free from fear and had broken the chains that had been binding me. Frequently, I did not know how long it would take me to walk to my destination as I was compelled to stop and ask anyone in my path if they knew Jesus. So, it was not long before I became involved with church outreach and street ministry. We had some glorious times worshipping with music outdoors in public places where crowds would gather as the Lord would bring His love and mercy and grace to whoever desired to come to Him. My heart is in the street with the destitute, the lost, and the lonely. The homeless often become invisible in a huge metropolis, but they do not go unnoticed by God!

> Isaiah 41:17 *The poor and needy seek water, but there is none, Their tongues fail for thirst. I, the LORD, will hear them; I, the God of Israel, will not forsake them.*

I was employed as a secretary in a large accounting firm in downtown Johannesburg. When I was hired for the position, the partner who I would be working with said to me, "All of the accountants in this firm are Jews except for me. Does that bother you?"

"Oh no," I replied, "I am Jewish myself." So now, three months later I was in his office telling him how Jesus had saved me. He truly thought that I had lost my mind. I also came to find out through some of the correspondence I did for him that he was a grand master in the freemasons.

I had heard amazing testimonies from Christians at church about how God had rescued them out of the most perilous crises. As I was walking to work on the busy streets of Johannesburg, I began to have day dreams of villains trying to do me harm. I would boldly declare, "In the Name of Jesus," and see them stopped in their tracks while I preached the Gospel to them, or they would turn and run away.

It happened that one day, during my lunch break, I found myself lost on a deserted downtown street while going to the bank to deposit some money. I was not afraid because I knew that God and His angels were with me. I had my handbag over my shoulder. It was one of those that had a flap that could flip open easily to put your hand inside. As I was standing at a corner trying to figure out where I was, a man came up to me and held a small piece of paper in front of my face with some writing on it. He asked me if I could tell him where a particular street was. I sensed the Holy Spirit telling me to look to the right and sure enough, another man was standing there holding my wallet and my bankbook. The power of God came over me as I said in a quiet authoritative tone, while taking back my belongings from his hand, "Give that to me, it's mine!" I don't know if those two men saw an angel but they both looked wide-eyed at me and turned and ran away faster than I could blink an eye.

Proverbs 3:25, 26 *Do not be afraid of sudden terror, nor of trouble from the wicked when it comes; for the Lord will be your confidence, and will keep your foot from being caught.*

Miraculously, I saw a familiar street sign that led me in the direction I needed to go. I could hardly wait to get back to the office to tell Mr. B about this as I had been praying for him and telling him about Jesus. *Surely,* I thought, *this will turn him around.* When I returned to work I ran into my boss's office and exclaimed, "Mr. B, Mr. B, I have to tell you what just happened!" The words describing the event tumbled out of my mouth like marbles being emptied from a bag one on top of the other.

"Oh, that must have been a terrible experience for you," he muttered.

"No, Mr. B, it was a WONDERFUL experience. God was with me!" I declared with excited enthusiasm.

With that, he peered at me over the top of his eye glasses and said in a firm, monotone voice; "Please, leave my office, NOW!"

A few days later, his teenage daughter came to see him, and after spending a few minutes in his office she ran out the door sobbing. I jumped up and hurried through the hallway and found her in the bathroom. She was crying uncontrollably, saying, "I hate him, I hate him." I put my arms around her and told her about the love of Jesus and invited her to come to church with me the following Sunday.

That Saturday night I had a vivid dream of Pastor Ray McCauley standing on the platform with his head and arms hanging down and looking at the rest of the music group but the worship leader was not there. The pastor took up a guitar and began to strum it very sadly.

On the way to church the next morning, I related this dream to the young woman and immediately after I had done so I thought, *Gosh, what have I done telling her about such a ridiculous dream?! She is going to think I am crazy!* Well, wouldn't you know it, as the service began the pastor got up on the platform looking melancholy as in my dream and announced that his worship leader had been called to minister in another province in South Africa and that he was going to be greatly missed. The girl and I looked at each other in amazement. Frankly, I was stunned.

She was born again that day and told me afterwards that the Bible she had at home had been her mother's, and all the Scriptures underlined were the ones read to her that morning! (Her mother had previously died of cancer.) Oh, what an awesome God we serve. Who can know the mind of God?

Reading the story in the Book of Matthew about Jesus cursing the fig tree ignited the gift of faith in me. As I had a noticeable skin colored mole on the front of my neck. I decided to take God at His Word. I spoke to the mole saying, "I curse you in the name of Jesus. I command you to wither up and die like the fig tree that Jesus cursed and to fall off of my neck!" The next morning when I glanced in the mirror, I noticed that the mole had turned dark black! Praise God, later that day it fell off!

Matthew 21:18-22 *Now in the morning, as He returned to the city, He was hungry. And seeing a fig tree by the road, He came to it and found nothing on it but leaves, and said to it, "Let no fruit grow on you ever again." Immediately the fig tree withered away.*

Chapter 13

> *And when the disciples saw it, they marveled, saying, "How did the fig tree wither away so soon?"*
>
> *So Jesus answered and said to them, "Assuredly, I say to you, if you have faith and do not doubt, you will not only do what was done to the fig tree, but also if you say to this mountain, 'Be removed and be cast into the sea,' it will be done. And whatever things you ask in prayer, believing, you will receive."*

I had an awesome supernatural experience one evening while leaving work in Johannesburg to get on the bus to take me home. The sky suddenly darkened and a heavy, pelting rain quickly turned into large hail stones. Along with the crowds, I took shelter in a department store. As I saw the time getting closer and closer to when I needed to catch my bus, I became concerned. There was only one bus and if I missed that, I would be stuck downtown with no transportation to get home to my children.

I asked God to protect me and I quickly left the store. I had no umbrella or anything to hold over myself. As I hurried along the pavement, God provided a supernatural covering over me until I reached the bus which had just arrived. Not a drop of rain or a hailstone touched me. I saw the rain and hail pouring down on others who were also making a mad dash for the bus! I am so overwhelmed with the goodness of my Heavenly Father who cares for the very hairs on my head!

> Luke 12:6-7 *Are not five sparrows sold for two copper coins? And not one of them is forgotten before God. But the very hairs of your head are all numbered. Do not fear therefore; you are of more value than many sparrows.*

There was no doubt in my mind that I needed to end my ungodly relationship with S. He was furious that I had taken the children to church and forbade us to return. When I ignored his order and rode the bus to church with Josie and Carl, he tried to intimidate me by following us in his car.

Once again, the Lord brought people into my life to help me. A young woman from the office offered to let us stay with her for a few days while I moved out of the apartment S and I had been sharing. Gwynn and his friend Ron helped me with our belongings while the children were at school and S was at work. I kept my key and after leaving, the first thing I did was to sneak back into the old apartment the next day. I wanted to get rid of the two pistols that S owned. It was during my lunch break and I was afraid that he might come after us as he was very manipulative and had tried to stop me from leaving him. So, there I was in the middle of Johannesburg carrying two loaded hand guns in my purse. Now that I had them, I was in a predicament as to what to do with them. If I buried them, someone might find them and commit a crime or worse still a murder! If I turned them in to the police, I might be charged with theft. This was a dilemma! I finally decided to continue trusting God to take care of me and my children since I certainly had a track record of getting myself in trouble. Knowing He had never failed to protect me in the past, I returned to the apartment, put the guns back where I had found them, and that was the end of it.

By this time, Psalm 91 had become very real to me. I read it almost daily, inserting "*me*" wherever it said "*you*" to make it personal.

Psalm 91
He who dwells in the secret place of the Most High
Shall abide under the shadow of the Almighty.
I will say of the LORD, "He is my refuge and my fortress;
My God, in Him I will trust."
Surely He shall deliver you from the snare of the fowler
And from the perilous pestilence.
He shall cover you with His feathers,
And under His wings you shall take refuge;
His truth shall be your shield and buckler.
You shall not be afraid of the terror by night,
Nor of the arrow that flies by day,

Chapter 13

Nor of the pestilence that walks in darkness,
Nor of the destruction that lays waste at noonday.

A thousand may fall at your side,
And ten thousand at your right hand;
But it shall not come near you.
Only with your eyes shall you look,
And see the reward of the wicked.

Because you have made the LORD, who is my refuge,
Even the Most High, your dwelling place,
No evil shall befall you,
Nor shall any plague come near your dwelling;
For He shall give His angels charge over you,
To keep you in all your ways.
In their hands they shall bear you up,
Lest you dash your foot against a stone.
You shall tread upon the lion and the cobra,
The young lion and the serpent you shall trample underfoot.

Because he has set his love upon Me, therefore I will deliver him;
I will set him on high, because he has known My name.
He shall call upon Me, and I will answer him;
I will be with him in trouble;
I will deliver him and honor him.
With long life I will satisfy him,
And show him My salvation.

A Christian nurse named Mary, whom I had met at a Bible study at Gwynn's home, kindly offered to let the children and me stay with her until I could find my own place. I can still see her as I write this. She was shorter than me with long, thick, straight dark brown hair, and large round blue eyes. She had rather fair skin and a few freckles on her face. Josie and Carl used to say that there was a beautiful scent of roses in her apartment. It was while we were living there that I experienced the baptism of the Holy Spirit.

My children were baptized in the Holy Spirit with the evidence of speaking in other tongues before I was and they used to say to me, "Mommy, Mommy, you need to speak in your heavenly language. It is a gift from God. It is not from the devil."

I Corinthians 14:2 *For he who speaks in a tongue does not speak to men but to God, for no one understands him; however, in the spirit he speaks mysteries.*

Acts 1:8 *But you shall receive power when the Holy Spirit has come upon you; and you shall be witnesses to Me in Jerusalem, and in all Judea and Samaria, and to the end of the earth.*

Acts 2:4 *And they were all filled with the Holy Spirit and began to speak with other tongues, as the Spirit gave them utterance.*

Matthew 21:16 *"Do You hear what these are saying?" And Jesus said to them, "Yes. Have you never read, 'Out of the mouth of babes and nursing infants You have perfected praise'?"*

The Israel-Lebanon conflict in 1982 weighed heavily on my heart. I didn't know how to pray about the situation, so when Josie and Carl were sleeping one night, I asked God to show me how to pray. Right there while I was sitting on the floor in the dark I began to speak in other tongues, for how long I do not know. Even though I was speaking in a language that my mind did not understand, I knew that I was praying about Israel and I knew I was declaring "Let my people go!"

> "In Lebanon, the fragile state of no-war, no-peace, in place since 1973, began to break down as the PLO strengthened its mini-state in Lebanon, established PLO military training centers, and escalated artillery and cross-border attacks on civilians in northern Israel. Israelis were forced to spend long periods of time in bomb shelters.
>
> The immediate trigger for Israel's operation into Lebanon was the attempted assassination of the Israeli ambassador in London on June 3, 1982. The next day, Israeli jets attacked PLO targets in Lebanon and the PLO responded with rocket and artillery barrages into northern Israel. The Israeli cabinet met to approve sending ground troops into Lebanon. Defense minister Ariel Sharon briefed the cabinet on "Operation Peace for Galilee" a plan for a limited incursion of twenty-five miles into Lebanon to wipe out PLO positions in southern Lebanon and thus safeguard Israel's population in northern Israel. The cabinet, including the opposition Labor Party, supported the plan for a limited operation."
> www.adl.org/Israel/record/lebanon.asp

Chapter 13

That was my first encounter with spiritual warfare. Afterwards, I woke the children and told them what had just happened and we danced and sang in celebration!

About three months later I was baptized in water (full immersion) and later, my children were also baptized in water. It was our public declaration of the death and burial of our old life and the resurrection to new life in Jesus Christ.

> Romans 6:3-5 *Or do you not know that as many of us as were baptized into Christ Jesus were baptized into His death? Therefore we were buried with Him through baptism into death, that just as Christ was raised from the dead by the glory of the Father, even so we also should walk in newness of life. For if we have been united together in the likeness of His death, certainly we also shall be in the likeness of His resurrection.*

The children and I found our own apartment in Hillbrow and, as usual, we had very little furniture. The building was anything but fancy, which was an advantage because the living room was so large that Josie and Carl were able to roller skate in it. It only took me about a half hour to walk to work from there. One of S's relatives lived in the apartment just above us. She had two children, Ricky and Nicky, who were around the same age as my two, so she was there to watch out for Josie and Carl when they came home from school. Little Nicky ran to me one day and excitedly quoted the Scripture from Romans 8:37 *We are more than conquerors through Him who loved us!* What a delight those children were to me!

One morning Josie and Carl were squabbling with each other while getting ready for school. I was feeling particularly inadequate that day to deal with life in general. I asked God, "Please give me a Scripture for today." Romans 12:1-2 immediately came to my mind. This Scripture became the plumb line with which to measure my walk with the Lord. In the scriptural sense, the plumb line is God's Word. God's Word is the standard to measure my life by. God's Word is Truth.

> Romans 12:1-2 *I beseech you therefore brethren, by the mercies of God, that you present your bodies a living sacrifice, holy, acceptable to God, which is your reasonable service. And do not be conformed to this world, but be transformed by the renewing of your mind, that you may prove what is that good and acceptable and perfect will of God.*

The next thing I knew that I had to do was to come clean with the South African authorities and tell them that I entered the country under false pretenses. Now, someone might say that it didn't matter because they had given me a work permit, but I wanted to be truthful about every part of my life. So Gwynn, the man who had taken me to church the first time kindly drove me to Pretoria to the government offices.

I told them that I needed to speak to someone in authority and that I had been dishonest about being a visitor to South Africa when my true intention was to live there permanently. I was ushered into an office and told to sit down. I was on one side of a large wooden table with a marble top and on the other side was a burly, heavy set Afrikaner. He looked at me and asked, "Why did you lie when you entered our country?"

I replied, "Because I did not know Jesus when I came here and I was afraid of the man I was with and did whatever he told me to do. But now, I know Jesus and I want to tell the truth because I am not afraid anymore."

He got up from his chair, marched back and forth behind his desk and said gruffly, "You Canadians think you can just come over here and do whatever you want! I don't know what to do with you. Wait here." As I waited, I wondered what would happen next.

The gentleman returned a few minutes later and directed me to go further down the hall to another office and sit. When I entered the room, it had a musty smell and the desk was piled high with stacks and stacks of papers. I thought no one was there until

Chapter 13

a quiet voice on the other side of the desk said, "So, you want to correct your status." Startled, I stretched my neck and peered through a space between two columns of papers to see a very thin, elderly gentleman with round spectacles sitting there. He had the kindest, most gentle face that I had ever seen and appeared to be dressed in a suit from the nineteenth century.

"Why, yes," I said. He stood up, pulled a book off the shelf behind him, and blew the dust off of it.

"Put your hand on this Bible and swear that what you are telling me is the truth."

"I can't swear. I am a Christian."

He looked a little exasperated and replied, "Alright, then, however you want to say it, just put your hand on this Bible and tell me that you are speaking the truth."

"Oh, yes," I said, "I am telling you the truth. I want to correct my status because Jesus has set me free." He then gave me some forms to sign and told me that I would be contacted by mail about my temporary residency. As Gwynn drove me back to Johannesburg, he told me that he had asked the Christians in his home Bible study to pray for me. Their prayers had been answered and I was overwhelmed once again by the grace and mercy of my Heavenly Father.

While walking home from work early one evening, I noticed a bakery. I thought it would be nice to surprise Josie and Carl with some pastries, so I hurried in just as the shop was closing. I had a very strong impression from the Holy Spirit to tell the lady behind the counter that "Jesus still loves you." There was one person ahead of me. Then they were gone and I was waiting to pay for my delicacies. In my mind, I was arguing with the Holy Spirit and asking, *Couldn't I just say Jesus loves you?* It didn't make sense to me to say, "Jesus STILL loves you," since I had never seen this woman before.

It was as if time stood still. I can remember standing there while everything seemed to be taking place in slow motion. It took forever for the lady to count my money and give me my change.

I finally blurted out, "God told me to say that Jesus still loves you!"

To my astonishment, she broke down and sobbed and finally was able to say, "I walked away from God some years ago and I thought that I had sinned so badly that I could never come back. Thank you so much for telling me that." I then told her what church I attended and that I hoped I would see her there. That experience really taught me that no matter how foolish or silly you might feel, if you believe the Holy Spirit is telling you to say something to someone, do it. A person's life could be hanging in the balance.

I Samuel 15:22 *To obey is better than sacrifice.*

An anniversary dinner was coming up at the church and, as I did not have an appropriate dress to wear to the event, I hadn't planned to attend. During a Sunday morning service someone passed me a note to meet a woman in the lobby after the meeting. This woman and I had never met, but she came up to me and told me that she did not know why but the Lord had impressed upon her to give me a dress. She had purchased it a few weeks before and knew that it was not for herself and was waiting on the Lord to show her who to give the dress to. That morning she saw me and knew that I was the one.

After church, the children and I accompanied her to her apartment to see this gift from the Lord. When I saw it hanging in the closet I knew that it was just perfect for me. It was an elegant black smock with long sleeves and a scoop neck. It had delicate strands of golden threads woven throughout the fabric to give it a shimmering affect. I tried it on and it fit me perfectly! I was overwhelmed to realize that the God of the universe would care so much for my every need, no matter how small and insignificant I might think it to be (Luke 12:7, Matthew 6:26).

Chapter 13

It was becoming more and more exciting to hear and obey the voice of the Holy Spirit. One day, an acquaintance presented me with a pair of shoes. I tried them on and they were not my size so I asked the Lord if they were meant for someone else. The next day I had a phone call from a friend who told me that they knew someone who desperately needed a pair of shoes and had no money to purchase them. I rushed right over and gave her the shoes for her friend. She later told me that they fit the girl as if they were made for her! I was learning to be attentive to the voice of the Holy Spirit.

Supernatural experiences were happening more frequently for me, such as the time I was walking home after attending a Bible study. I realized that I was lost in an unfamiliar neighborhood. I asked the Holy Spirit to guide me, and before I knew it, I was on my own street! I had no idea how I got there except that I was led by the Lord. How awesome is our God!

The church was holding a retreat, and once again, I was not planning to attend. It was for adults only, and I did not have anyone I felt comfortable leaving my children with. Again, the Lord provided. A Christian sister I trusted approached me and said she would love to have my son and daughter over to visit for the weekend so that I could go to the retreat. The day before I was to leave, I had a terrible headache while at work. There was an older woman in the office who was a massage therapist and she offered to give me a back and neck massage. When she did so she told me that my spine was slightly crooked and that was why I was having problems with headaches.

I had a terrible headache the whole weekend and on Sunday morning I asked for prayer. A young preacher prayed for me and I went and sat down. I still had a throbbing headache. We were all seated in a circle on chairs and he was praying for a lady beside me. He asked her to stretch out her legs and one leg was shorter than the other. To my amazement, when he prayed for her, her shorter leg lengthened and became the same as the other leg. He then turned to me and asked if I still had pain in my head and neck. I told him I did and he asked me to also stretch out my legs. There it was, my right leg was noticeably shorter than my left one. He started to pray and even before he put his hand on my leg, it began to lengthen from the knee down. I was so excited that I began jumping up and down praising God. It was only days later that I remembered wearing brown oxfords as a child and then, as a teenager attempting to sit so my feet would be even with each other. My children had even commented to me at times that I walked funny, but I had never really paid much attention to any of these things until I was healed that day.

When I returned to the office on Monday, I asked the lady who had given me the massage to have a look at my back. I was sure that the Lord had straightened that too. To her surprise, she could see nothing wrong. She said, "Your spine is straight! I must have made a mistake." I told her that Jesus had healed me and I left the rest up to the Holy Spirit. She insisted that my spine had been straight all along. I had planted the seed and perhaps someone else would be the one to reap the harvest.

I was soon to attend my first Passover Seder. (The word "Seder" is a Hebrew word meaning "Order". It refers to the ritual presentation of Passover.)

A lady that I had met at church found out that I was Jewish and offered to take me to a Seder, revealing Yeshua (Jesus) as the Jewish Messiah. It was in Johannesburg and the group conducting it may have been from Jews for Jesus.

The Passover is observed each year by Jews all over the world to give thanks to God for His deliverance of the children of Israel from the bondage of slavery in Egypt. After Pharaoh had refused to let the Hebrews go, God declared a tenth plague which was the death of the firstborn of every family in Egypt (Exodus 11). God gave Moses instructions for the children of Israel to keep death from their homes on that night of judgment (Exodus 12:1-14, 43-48). A lamb was to be slaughtered for each household and the blood was to be applied to the doorposts of the home. The entire lamb was to be roasted and eaten with nothing left over. As the Hebrews remained in their dwellings, the plague passed over them, because of the blood on their doorposts, and they were saved.

We know as believers in the Messiah that Jesus is the Lamb of God who was slain from the foundation of the world (Revelation 13:8; 1 Peter 1:20: Isaiah 53). His blood was poured out once and for all. He is not a High Priest who needs to come yearly to make atonement for our transgressions. By His death and resurrection he ever lives to make intercession for us (Hebrews 9:12). Only those in covenant with God, with the outward sign of circumcision, were allowed to participate in the consuming of the slain and roasted lamb. We, who are believers in Yeshua (Jesus), have been circumcised in our hearts (Romans 2:28-29).

Since I had never attended a Passover Seder before, I had nothing to compare this one with. The entire event was a rich spiritual experience for me of giving thanks and praise to the Most High God for saving me.

At the Seder that night, a young man named Kevin was chosen to ask the traditional question, "Why is this night different than any other night?" A child is usually chosen for this but there were no children present. Kevin was the youngest man there, being about eighteen years old.

While conversing throughout the evening, Kevin asked me if I would accompany him to visit an elderly Jewish man who he had been sharing his faith with. I was more than happy to oblige. About a week later, he picked me up, and we drove to the gentleman's apartment. After spending about an hour there, we left and, Kevin exclaimed to me, "I can't believe it! I have been visiting this guy for months, going through all the Old Testament prophecies with him. I was brought up in a strict Jewish home and have all this knowledge of the Scriptures. I take you along and you just walk into this man's room and ask him right off, 'Do you know Jesus?' The amazing thing is that now he wants to know more about Jesus!" So, for a short while, Kevin and I were a great witnessing team—me with my enthusiasm and Kevin with the Scriptures to verify the Truth. If I remember correctly, not too long after that, he went back to North America to be with his father.

During that same year, I was privileged to attend a meeting in a small church in Johannesburg where Reinhard Bonke was speaking. I was sitting in the front row and I was deeply moved by his passion for the vision God had given him for lost souls and of the continent of Africa being washed in the precious blood of Jesus. He had a zeal for God that was contagious! That night, I was ignited with a fresh passion in my heart for the lost. In another small church, I was praying along with another person for a young man on crutches and when the power of God touched him, he threw down his crutches and began jumping up and down declaring that he was healed of a broken leg! Don't tell me that Jesus doesn't do miracles today. I have seen and experienced it myself!

Later that year, Gwynn took me to a meeting at a church called Faith City where Benny Hinn was preaching. For the life of me, I could not understand what he meant by "Faith City" as I was not familiar with Christian churches. In my mind, I envisioned a city. When I asked him what this Faith City was, he just replied that it was a place where Christian brothers and sisters got together and worshipped God. But, I wanted to know if they all lived together. I thought it might be some kind of a commune. He gazed at me with a not-knowing-what-to-make-of-me look and said that I would see when we got there. Well, we arrived, and to my surprise there was a large church building with a sign on the front that said, "Faith City."

The auditorium was packed and we were at the very back, but I could see Benny on the platform. I remember that he was teaching about fasting and prayer, but the only thing I can really recall

Chapter 13

is seeing him on his knees crawling across the platform. He was talking about the temptations that came whenever he attempted to fast and pray. He spoke of having sudden hunger pangs while a giant hamburger or milkshake would appear in his mind's eye to distract him. Such was my second introduction to spiritual warfare, the first being when I was baptized in the Holy Spirit and prayed in other tongues about the Israel-Lebanon conflict. Actually, his demonstration was quite powerful as it impacted my heart and mind by bringing understanding about the battle we wage between the spirit and the flesh. *I say then, walk in the spirit and you will not fulfill the lust of the flesh* (Galations 5:16).

While the children and I were living in our apartment in Hillbrow, we saw spiritual warfare put into action. The three of us were sick with flu-like symptoms for a couple of weeks and couldn't seem to get better. One day, while I was home from work and Josie and Carl home from school, an elderly couple knocked at our door. When I answered, they told me that God had sent them to us because we were sick. I asked them in and one of them said, "You have something from the occult in this apartment and that is why you are sick." I had no idea what they were talking about because I had no knowledge yet of those things. They noticed a pair of bongo drums on my table and said "That's it. Where did you get those? They have been used in witchcraft. You need to get rid of them!" I had purchased them in Zimbabwe and brought them with us to South Africa. The Holy Spirit told me to do as they said. We took them out to the garbage. The couple prayed for us and I renounced any previous involvement with the occult and broke curses from past generations. They left and the next morning the children and I woke up totally free of any sickness! I had never seen those people before and never saw them again after that event. Were they angels? *Do not forget to entertain strangers, for by so doing some have unwittingly entertained angels* (Hebrews 13:2).

II Corinthians 10:4,5 *For the weapons of our warfare are not carnal but mighty in God for pulling down strongholds, casting down arguments and every high thing that exalts itself against the knowledge of God, bringing every thought into captivity to the obedience of Christ.*

CHAPTER 14

"The Child Came Running"

After living in Hillbrow for a while, I heard that a lady in the church named Magda was looking for someone to share her cottage with her. I jumped at the opportunity, as it would be in a better neighborhood and closer to the church. By this time, we had acquired a little tortoiseshell kitten that we brought along. Magda had an adorable fluffy, white miniature poodle and it appeared that our kitten began to think she was a dog, too. She used to run to the end of the walkway to see the children off to school and then go out to meet them when they came home!

We lived in that cottage for about three months when circumstances caused us to move yet again. We were offered a place to stay with the children's ministry leaders. Colin and Cheryl were a lovely young couple dedicated to the Lord. They owned a beautiful house on a large property across from a creek that was lined with trees. Another young lady from our church rented a room in the house along with us. We used to come together to pray in the early morning hours before our schedules became busy. Those were very special times for me.

During school vacation while living with Colin and Cheryl, Josie, Carl and I accompanied another single mother with her two children to the South Coast. Our destination was Kwa Zulu, Natal Province, to a town called Margate. We stayed in a trailer which South Africans call a caravan. On the Sunday morning before we were to return to Johannesburg, we attended a small church, also called Faith City. This time I knew that "Faith City" was the name of a church. During the service I noticed that all the children were in the meeting, and I felt a very strong impression that the Holy Spirit was telling me that we were to move to Margate where I was to start a children's ministry. I was already involved in the Chil-

Chapter 14

dren's Ministry at Rhema, as a helper, so I shared my desire with the pastor before we left. He gave me the church's phone number and we both decided to take it to the Lord in prayer.

When we returned to Johannesburg, I sought counsel from Colin and Cheryl. They asked me if I would be receiving a salary and I said I had never considered that, but if God called me to do this, He would provide. I truly believed that with all my heart. After a few calls back and forth to the pastor in Margate, and a time of seeking the Lord's will in prayer, I made the decision to move down there.

I gave my notice at the office where I was working as a secretary, and it was arranged for Josie, Carl, and me to stay temporarily with an older retired couple who attended the church in Margate. Their names were Petra and Meent. I remember Meent as a quiet man who seemed to be content to pursue his hobby of making jewelry. Petra was a very straight forward, bold Christian. It was only when we arrived at her home that she told me that the church had been praying for the Lord to send someone to start a Children's Ministry. The day that I first visited, she knew that it should be me. The Lord always confirms His Word!

The night before we left Johannesburg, I had a dream that I remember clearly to this day. In my dream, I was walking along a beach front that had rows and rows of buildings with many windows in each structure. There was water rushing, as it were, from behind the buildings through the windows and out the front. The water poured out in torrents for some time and then it stopped. I found myself in front of one of the buildings, and there was a very tall man beside me. Whether he was a man or an angel, I do not know. He was dressed in white and must have been at least seven feet tall because I could not see his face. He took me inside (I honestly do not remember if he spoke at that point). We went up a winding staircase and on the landings to the next level were carved idols. I asked him, "But where are all the people?"

Then, I was immediately walking along the beach with my

children on each side of me. The man said to us, "Fear not, our house is safe." When I awoke, I knew that the children and I had found our place of refuge in Him, the Lord of Lords, the King of Kings, the Alpha and Omega, the beginning and the end. Yeshua would be our shelter from the storm.

Proverbs 12:7 *The wicked are overthrown and are no more, but the house of the righteous will stand.*

Proverbs 1:33 *But whoever listens to me will dwell safely, and will be secure, without fear of evil.*

A friend drove us to Margate from Johannesburg and, of course, we brought our kitten. It was quite a trip and I had to put her on a leash during the night so we could take her out to do her business. Petra was not too thrilled about us bringing a cat into her house but I did not have the heart to make the children part with her. We settled in and I went out to search for work. There was nothing in the newspaper, so when I arrived in town, which was about a half-hour walk from our residence, I said, "Lord, I know You called me here, so I know that You will provide for me and my children. Please show me, Holy Spirit, where to look for employment." I started walking and felt prompted to go to a red brick building on the corner. I entered and went up one flight of stairs to what turned out to be a law office. I told the receptionist that I was new in town and had administrative experience and would like to know if they were hiring anyone at the present time.

"Oh my goodness!" she exclaimed. "You won't believe this. I was just about to put an ad in the paper for a clerk typist. Just wait here a minute and I will call the boss and see if he would like to speak to you." I had an interview right then and there, and they hired me to start on the Monday of the following week!

Every time we moved, it broke my heart that Josie and Carl had to start all over again in a new school. I know that this was not easy for either of them. A few years ago I told my daughter how sorry I was that I had moved them around so much while

Chapter 14

growing up. She said, "Mom, living in different countries was the best part of my life." Carl told me that it gave him so much more maturity and broader horizons compared to other teenagers he met when we returned to Canada. My children are a true gift from the Lord!

After living with Petra and Meent for a few months, a married couple in the church (Lettie was the wife's name) said that they had a caravan we could stay in until I was able to find a place of our own. So, again, we packed our few belongings along with our tortoiseshell kitten and moved to the caravan park. This was a short walking distance from church and also near my place of work. The school bus picked up the children. There was no public transportation. Now, I wished I had not given up so soon when a lady friend in Zimbabwe had attempted to teach me to drive while I had been living there. I gave up after only two lessons. In any case, I had no finances to purchase a vehicle.

The first emergency we experienced after moving in was that our kitten disappeared. Josie and Carl were terribly distraught as we looked everywhere but could not find her. We prayed and asked the Holy Spirit to help us. Then, in the quiet of the evening we heard a faint meow coming from somewhere in our caravan. We traced the sound to a storage unit that, when closed, served as a bench to sit on. When we opened it, there she was, amongst the bedding and towels. She must have jumped in and curled up and gone to sleep without anyone noticing. What joy we had when we found her. Unfortunately, she got us in trouble with the management on a regular basis because that park was a bird sanctuary and she used to chase the birds, trying to catch them. The two elderly sisters who owned the park said that their two cats didn't do that and, frankly, we could see why. Their cats were so old and fat that they could only dream of climbing a tree. So, I promised to try to keep charge of our kitty as best I could.

The trailer next to us housed an elderly couple. The wife didn't seem to go out of her abode very often, but the husband was a kind and friendly gentleman. He noticed that I did not have a car, so he offered to help me out by taking me to buy groceries on the weekends. I spoke to him about Jesus, and he asked me to please not talk to his wife about such things. He said she conducted séances in their caravan at night, and there were even occasions when the table would rise and she would talk to the dead.

I did not have an opportunity to speak with her until one evening when we were both washing our clothes in the communal laundry. We exchanged greetings and she told me that she was suffering from a terrible migraine headache. Not to miss an opportunity, I told her about Jesus the Healer and asked if I could pray for her. She declined my offer and left my presence very quickly.

That night, I had a dream. In my dream a warlock was coming towards me with a knife and was going to cut out my heart. I awoke abruptly and immediately knew that it had something to do with the lady next door. I prayed for her salvation. In the morning, I told my children about my dream and they both said, "Mommy, Mommy, the devil wants your heart. Don't give it to him."

For some time I did not see the man next door or his wife. Finally, one day I noticed him standing outside his caravan and I asked him how his wife was doing. He became visibly agitated and said that she had died a terrible death and it was such that he could not even talk about it. I was shocked and humbled by that experience. We never know when we speak to someone about Jesus how close or how far their time to depart from this life will be.

While living in that caravan park, another elderly man approached me and asked right out, "Will you go to bed with me?"

I immediately replied, "You don't need me, you need Jesus!"

He said, "Oh, I am a satan worshipper." He never approached me again after I mentioned the name of Jesus to him.

The time came when Lettie and her husband needed their caravan back. I found an apartment which was a separate building off of a large house that the landlord and his family lived in.

Chapter 14

I had a different office job by then and my desk was in front of a window that had an excellent view of the sea. Often I would watch the dolphins leaping and diving in the water. This office was within walking distance of our new dwelling and the children's school. Josie and Carl used to come to my workplace after school and sit and do their homework. Then we would walk home together.

This region was home to little black and white Vervet monkeys. They hop from tree to tree the way squirrels do here in North America. Quite amazingly, if our little cat sat outside of our doorway, the monkeys would keep their distance as if she was a huge lion or tiger. It was quite amazing.

This office downsized and once again I found new employment. This time it was in an insurance office. We also needed to move again because mold was forming on the walls due to dampness and poor construction of the building we were living in.

My supervisor at work was very critical of me. It seemed that nothing I said or did would make her happy. It was then that I remembered Pastor Ray preaching about blessing those who persecute you (Romans 12:1), so I thought that I would give it a try. I ordered a bouquet of flowers from the local florist and had it delivered to her at the office with a card from me. I was taken by surprise by her reaction the next morning when it arrived. She burst into tears and said that no one had ever done anything like that for her before. We became good friends after that and she shared a little about her life with me. I came to know that she was going through an extremely difficult situation with her grown son.

We must never be quick to judge by outward appearances. We often don't know what is going on in a person's life to make them act the way they do.

I Samuel 16:7 *But the LORD said to Samuel, "Do not look at his appearance or at his physical stature, because I have refused him. For the LORD does not see as man sees; for man looks at the outward appearance, but the LORD looks at the heart".*

> Matthew 7:1-5 *Judge not, that you be not judged. For with what judgment you judge, you will be judged; and with the measure you use, it will be measured back to you. And why do you look at the speck in your brother's eye, but do not consider the plank in your own eye? Or how can you say to your brother, 'Let me remove the speck from your eye'; and look, a plank is in your own eye? Hypocrite! First remove the plank from your own eye, and then you will see clearly to remove the speck from your brother's eye.*

When my supervisor found out that I was moving again, she organized the office employees and they purchased a sofa and table and chairs that were secretly put into our apartment before we moved in. What a surprise when the children and I arrived and saw the furniture with a note welcoming us to our new home. I was overwhelmed by their kindness because all we really had to our name were beds and a couple of dressers. The following two Scriptures became very real to me that day.

> Romans 12:21 *Do not be overcome by evil, but overcome evil with good.*
>
> Romans 2:4 *Or do you despise the riches of His goodness, forbearance and longsuffering, not knowing that the goodness of God leads you to repentance?*

After attending the church in Margate for a few months, Pastor Albert Fryer felt that it was time for me to begin the Children's Ministry. I was excited and apprehensive at the same time. I didn't know how to do this except to pray and seek the Lord for guidance. So there we were, about twenty-five children, including mine, on our first Sunday. There was a young man named David in the church who was interested in helping with the worship, so he brought along his guitar. David later taught me how to play the guitar so that I, too, could lead worship with an instrument.

While we were at Rhema Bible Church in Johannesburg, a children's evangelist, Willie George (Gospel Bill), had visited. I was really taken with his teachings and had sent away for some

Chapter 14

materials which I now found very helpful. After a time of worship during that first morning, I asked if there were any children needing prayer. Several came to the front. The first one was a little boy of about seven years old. He just kept pointing to his ear. I didn't know if he had an earache or what was the matter, because he could not speak English. After asking the Holy Spirit how to pray, I commanded a spirit of infirmity to leave in the name of Jesus. Immediately, the little boy ran out of the children's room and into the sanctuary to where his parents were. I thought maybe I had frightened him!

We continued with the service. When we were finished and the parents had all picked up their children, Miriam, the pastor's wife, came to me. She told me how excited everyone had been about the little Afrikaans boy who had been healed in the children's church that morning. I asked, "What do you mean?"

She said, "Rhonda, that child you prayed for had been deaf in one ear since birth and he came running to his parents to tell them that he could hear out of that ear!"

"Not by might nor by power, but by My Spirit," Says the LORD of hosts (Zechariah 4:6).

After leading the Children's Ministry for about one year there was a need to train more workers because more children were attending. I was shocked at myself as I became very possessive of the ministry. The pastor had to tell me to stop sitting at the back of the class when the trainees were teaching because I was making them nervous. I really had to let go and realize that this was God's ministry, not mine. It had been a glorious time of growing in the Lord together with the children. Many times I would prepare a lesson for Sunday morning and afterwards find out that the pastor had preached a similar message to the adult congregation. There is nothing more exciting than walking with the Lord. The things of this world cannot compare.

For the first few years of my journey with Jesus, I totally

stopped watching television, reading the newspaper or listening to the radio. I would not tell others to do this. It was for me because I was walking in fear and I needed to saturate myself with the Word of God rather than the bad reports of the world. It was not a legalistic thing. It was a prompting by the Holy Spirit.

At one of our prayer meetings at the church in Margate I felt that the Lord had given me a word to speak, but I had never done anything like that before. So, after the meeting, I told Pastor Fryer about it. He very firmly told me that I should have spoken it out and that if I felt prompted again at our next prayer meeting, I should do so.

During the next meeting as we were all in a circle praying, the Holy Spirit prompted me again, so I delivered the word from the Lord, "*Do you not know that your body is a temple of the Holy Spirit?*" I had my eyes closed and I heard one thud after another as several of the youth fell backward onto the floor being immediately slain in the Spirit. I later found out that each one who had been touched by the Lord had been delivered that night from cigarette smoking! So, there you go. I had no knowledge of their lives and certainly did not have any idea of the impact that word would have. Once again, we just need to be willing vessels and simply obey the voice of the Holy Spirit, and God will take care of the need, whatever it is.

"Josie, Carl, I just received a letter from your Aunt Gilda. She is going to visit us for Christmas!" The children were excited that she was coming. I was really looking forward to seeing my sister because I had mailed her some Christian music tapes from Rhema Church in Johannesburg the previous year. I had also included a letter telling her I was "born again" and asking her to forgive me for any hurt I had caused her in the past. I'm not positive, but I believe this was the first time I had heard from her since that letter.

Our apartment was above a video and grocery store facing onto a courtyard. Adelle, a young single mom from our church, lived in the apartment directly across from us with her six year

Chapter 14

old daughter. She owned a car and offered to take my sister, the children, and me on a trip to Durban where we enjoyed a wonderful day at the beach. Gil brought Christmas stockings and hung them on our wall. She also insisted on purchasing new clothes for Josie and Carl. She came to church with us once. When I raised my hands to praise the Lord, she tugged at my arm and asked what I was doing. I had forgotten how strange it felt to be in a church service before being touched by the Holy Spirit. She was especially concerned when I put my tithe in the offering basket as it was passed around. She actually grabbed my arm and tried to stop me! It was no use trying to explain. I knew she wouldn't understand. We were invited, along with several others, to have Christmas lunch at the home of one of the families of the congregation. Gil was very uneasy that day. She really thought that I had joined a cult!

One evening I left her with the children while I attended a meeting. When I came home she was sitting in our kitchen with her feet on the table while Josie and Carl were sleeping in their bedrooms. "What are you doing?" I asked.

"There's a mouse in here and I am not putting my feet down until you find it!" Poor Gil! A mouse was the least of my concerns, but I decided not to discuss cockroaches and snakes with her. Anyway, I looked all over for that mouse and finally said we should go to sleep because I was sure it was not in our apartment anymore. I was just drifting off into a deep slumber when I heard Gil's voice quietly saying, "Rhonda, Rhonda."

"What now?" I asked.

"Rhonda, the mouse is in my beach bag beside my bed!"

"Don't be ridiculous!" I replied.

"Rhonda, please take my beach bag outside." So, to pacify her and to get some sleep, I picked up the bag and as I stood at the front door to open it, a face stared up at me from inside the bag and I was so startled that I shrieked and dropped it, opened the door, and shoved it outside.

Now Gil really couldn't settle down so I decided to make us a cup of tea. You have to picture this. I was sitting with my back to the kitchen window and Gil was sitting across from me on the other side of the table facing the window. All of a sudden, she put down her cup and her eyes became as large as saucers as she stared at me and pointed. She was in such a state of shock that she couldn't speak. I heard a thumping on the window behind me and when I turned to look, there was our cat with the mouse hanging from her mouth banging on the window wanting to come in!

So, back to the bedroom we went to get my sister calmed down again. I had just fallen asleep when I heard a screech. This time, Josie and Carl woke up too and came running to our room. "Oh no, what is it now?" I yelled.

"Something's in my hair, something's in my hair!" she screamed. Gil's dark brown hair was a mass of thick curls. A stink bug had flown into it and was stuck. Josie came to the rescue with a bucket. She took the bug out of her Aunt's hair and placed the bucket over it on the floor where it finally suffocated. Gil's final words before going to sleep that night were, "The next time I take a vacation, I am going to the North Pole!"

After Gil returned to Canada, I unexpectedly received a letter from the South African government stating that my temporary residency had run out and the children and I would have to leave. It came as quite a shock. I gathered together with some brothers and sisters in the church and we prayed for God to overturn the decision. Amazingly, it happened, but I was to realize later that I should not have interfered with the Lord's plans for me and my children. Our church had taken on an assistant pastor named Sandy. When he found out about what I had done, he told me that I was out of the will of God. His words of correction angered me as I mistakenly thought it would be wrong to leave a ministry I had started and to uproot my children again. It turned out that Sandy was right because I then took a turn that I never thought I would take.

Chapter 14

I took my eyes off of Jesus and began to look at the circumstances surrounding me and my children. I started to feel inadequate as a parent because of finances, even though God had always provided for us in miraculous ways. I felt that my children needed a father like the rest of their schoolmates. Instead of putting my trust in Abba Father, I once again took my life and the lives of my children into my own hands.

This makes me think of Exodus 24:9-11 when Moses took Aaron, Nadab and Abihu and seventy of the elders of Israel up with him. The Scripture tells us that they saw God and they ate and drank there. Yet later, in Exodus 32, when Moses was up on the mountain for forty days receiving instructions from God to build the tabernacle, the children of Israel became tired of waiting for Moses and they convinced Aaron to build the golden calf.

I met "M" in the church and I allowed myself to be charmed while He played the guitar, romancing me. If I had obeyed the Lord and left South Africa when I received that letter, I never would have married M who was an alcoholic and who caused much emotional pain in our lives. He moved us into a cottage by the sea and our troubles began immediately as he drank all our money away. I struggled to put food on the table and supply Josie and Carl with the clothes and books they needed for school.

One night M came home drunk and forgot to lock the front door before he flopped down to sleep. I was awakened by voices. I opened my eyes to see a strange man standing over me with a knife pointed towards me. I sat up with a jolt and stared at him. I was dumbfounded and unable to speak. Then, he appeared to gaze upwards and past me with a look of sheer terror on his face as his eyes bulged and his mouth opened wide. He turned and bolted out the front door. I believe that he must have seen a warrior angel because I looked and no one was there.

Psalm 91:11 *For He shall give His angels charge over you, to keep you in all your ways.*

Shortly after that, Josie showed up one day on a motorcycle with a friend from school who had given her two Rottweiler/Labrador mix puppies. She and Carl named them Brandy and Red. After having the experience with a break-in, I was not about to complain about having a couple of dogs around. By that time, we had acquired another cat which was part wild cat. It used to jump almost as high as the ceiling to catch the little lizards that would crawl up on our walls. Carl saved that cat's life one day when one of the puppies had it in his mouth and went running outside. Those dogs used to eat absolutely anything! One day a fisherman came chasing after Josie on the beach because the dogs had gotten away from her and eaten all of his fishing bait!

Once, Carl brought two tiny white mice home from school for the weekend. His friend had asked him to look after them. I exclaimed to my son, "Carl, you should have asked my permission before agreeing to such a responsibility. You know we have a cat. He will eat those mice!"

He replied, "It's okay, Mom. They are in a box with holes for air. I'll keep them safe." The next day I was chasing around the house after our cat which had one of them in its mouth, and I couldn't believe I was rescuing a mouse! Miraculously, I was able to free the little creature and I think Carl learned that our home was not a good environment for tiny white mice.

In 1986, I received another letter from the government and this one told me that I had to leave the country within a few weeks. I was stunned! I asked them what would happen if I didn't have the necessary funds, and they said that I would have to go to prison until I could prove I was not able to purchase a plane ticket. I certainly could not rely on M for help. I called my brother Stan in Toronto and he, Gilda, and Larry got together and purchased plane tickets for the children and me to return to Canada immediately. I can't express how thankful I am to my family who came to my aid without a moment's hesitation.

Chapter 14

Leaving South Africa was especially painful for my daughter Josie, who was fifteen years old and in the second year of high school. She was an avid surfer and had many friends. Her closest girlfriend Tracy was like a second daughter to me and my heart was aching as I saw her forlorn face while she stood there watching us leave to go to the airport. The emotional pain for Josie was such that she couldn't even speak. On the other hand, Carl being fourteen and in his first year of high school, was looking forward to seeing snow again. His most vivid memory of Canada was that of a winter wonderland. What had been weighing heavily on my mind for the past year was that at age eighteen he would be called up for active duty in the south African army for two years. Part of his grade nine curriculum consisted of military training to prepare him for service.

During the few years that we lived there, South Africa was in a border war with South West Africa (now Namibia) which lasted from 1966 until 1989. During our final year from 1985 to 1986, a "State of Emergency" had been declared by the South African Government which meant organizations and meetings could be banned and people who were suspected of political unrest against Apartheid could be detained at random. During this time, thousands of people were detained and media coverage of areas of unrest banned.

Being electronically scanned before entering a grocery store or a mall had become part of everyday life for us. Upon arriving at school, the children had to leave their book bags on the floor outside of their lockers. I found it difficult to come to terms with the fact that I was living a privileged life as a white person in South Africa. I wondered, Should I just take my children and leave or should I remain as my friend Jenny did in Zimbabwe when she told me, "God told the Christians to stay, so we are staying!"? I had been waiting on God to show me what to do when my answer came in the most unexpected way; in the form of this order to leave the country. Wherever we find ourselves as believers, we are to be salt and light to a dying world. We are to stand up for justice and do what is right in God's eyes. I did not become involved politically. However, I did become involved spiritually through prayer, outreach and friendships to all people, regardless of race or color.

>Matthew 5:13-15 *You are the salt of the earth; but if the salt loses its flavor, how shall it be seasoned? It is then good for nothing but to be thrown out and trampled underfoot by men. You are the light of the world. A city that is set on a hill cannot be hidden. Nor do they light a lamp and put it under a basket, but on a lampstand, and it gives light to all who are in the house.*

At the airport, as we were going through the gate, a guard asked me why we were leaving South Africa. This question gave Josie the perfect opportunity to release her frustration, anger and pain as she exclaimed loudly, "Because you are kicking us out of your country!" The guard looked a little surprised, and I felt my face turn crimson as we continued along the ramp to board our flight.

>Matthew 28:20 *"… And and lo, I am with you always, even to the end of the age."*
>
>Hebrews 13:5 *… For He Himself has said, "I will never leave you nor forsake you."*

CHAPTER 15

"Lady, Take Your Chances."

Our journey back to Canada from South Africa was a very long one with a full day's stop at Heathrow airport in London before boarding another plane for Toronto. When we saw all the men walking around wearing dark suits with white shirts and dark ties, Josie and Carl said, "Gee Mom, they all look like penguins!" After living in Africa, we were used to seeing men wearing safari suits and the clothing for women was so much more colorful in comparison to what appeared to us to be drab and plain here in Britain and later in North America.

We were exhausted from traveling. On our flight from Margate, South Africa, we had mistakenly been seated in the smoking section. I insisted that they move us. They did, but it turned out to be worse because the only other seats available were three at the very back of our section against a wall. This meant that we could not recline our chairs to be more comfortable. To make matters worse, the smoking section was the row directly to the left of us, as if the smoke would be able to stay on the other side of the isle! When my dear sister Gilda met us at the Toronto airport, I hardly recognized her. She had dyed her hair blonde.

It was an experience of culture shock for us returning to a big city like Toronto. We had been transported from a majestic landscape of lush gardens, full of multi-colored blossoms, contrasted by the thunderous sound of waves of the sea crashing up against gigantic rocks. As my brother Stan drove us from the airport, everything appeared dull and dreary to me. It was unusually hot for the month of May. The only colors I could see were brown/gray buildings, dirty sidewalks, and green trees and grass. I didn't see the rainbow of colors that I was used to. My brother pointed

Chapter 15

out some recently constructed skyscrapers that he thought were magnificent examples of architecture. I thought they looked like concrete monstrosities. As we passed a high school, Gil piped up, "Look children, you'll soon be going to a school like that!"

"Don't mention that now!" I sternly said. I could only imagine how Josie and Carl must be feeling. They were used to attending schools that were low rise and newly built, surrounded by lush green fields. Here was an old dinosaur of a brick building in the middle of downtown Toronto surrounded by other ugly buildings on busy concrete streets.

Our first night sleeping at Gilda's apartment at Yonge St. and St. Clair Ave. was challenging. The decibels of the constant drone of traffic were magnified in my senses as I attempted to re-adjust to the sights and sounds of the city. We hadn't lived in a large metropolis for more than three years. As I lay down that night, I concentrated my thoughts on remembering the soothing rhythm of the waves of the sea in Margate, and the refreshing salt water breezes brushing across my face. I finally fell into a deep slumber only to wake up to the reality of the dust and clamor of the city the next morning. Rather than thanking God for bringing us safely home, I cried with self pity to the Lord, "How could you do this? How could you bring us back to Toronto? You know I never wanted to come back here!" Oh, what a rebellious child I was. Even as I was complaining, I knew in my heart that His plans for me are for good and not for evil and that I should just put my trust in Him.

As difficult as this change was for me, it was more so for the children. Josie had loved surfing and Carl had been sailing with his friend before we left. One thing I did after we were somewhat settled was to take them to the Toronto waterfront on Lake Ontario where they took lessons in windsurfing. It didn't take the place of surfing and sailing on the sea, but I had hoped it would help a little to ease my son and daughter back into life in the city.

The first task Gil felt she had was to get us all some new clothes. I guess the three of us must have looked pretty bedraggled. We were used to living by the sea and other than school uniforms, the children had mostly T-shirts and shorts and we wore flip flops on our feet. We walked downhill from her apartment toward "The Bay" department store. It seemed that she and everyone else on the street were walking so fast. We were not accustomed to that pace anymore. In Margate, South Africa, our lives were lived less frantically, even when we lived in a large city like Johannesburg. There, friends just dropped in on each other because not everyone had a telephone.

We found some acceptable clothing for Toronto and the next thing I did was to look in the newspaper to find a church for us to attend. What a shock! There were lists of Evangelical, Pentecostal, Charismatic, along with all the usual denominations such as Baptist, Protestant, Lutheran, etc. I had no idea what I was supposed to do. In South Africa, I was not familiar with different categories except for the mainline churches. If they referred to themselves in those terms, I had no knowledge of it. All I knew was that I was born again by the Spirit of God, and I had a relationship with Jesus.

As I continued to scan the newspaper, I noticed a church called Evangel Temple which was close to Gil's apartment on the subway line. I decided to visit the Sunday of that week to see what God might show me. At this point, my son and daughter were not interested in coming to church with me. As I entered the lobby, I was greeted by friendly and loving brothers and sisters in the Lord. The worship music was similar to what I had experienced in the South African churches.

I cannot explain why, but it was during this time that the anxiety attacks returned. I remember having to be careful to seat myself at the back of the auditorium so I would be under a low ceiling. Once again, I was afraid to tell anyone about it. Nevertheless, this did not prevent me from becoming involved with an

Chapter 15

outreach ministry in the church. We would meet together on a Friday evening and pray before taking the subway downtown where we went out in two's or three's to share the Gospel and to pray with anyone who desired or needed prayer.

After living with Gilda for a short while in her small apartment, my brother Stan offered to have us come to live with him in his three-storey house until I found a place for us. Someone in the leadership at Evangel Temple had found out about our plight and I was overwhelmed and blessed when they told me they would pay our first month's rent as soon as I found an apartment. I managed to find work with a temporary agency and my first assignment was at a new complex downtown called Canada Place. I was totally mesmerized by the enormity of the building which took up a whole city block. During my first lunch break, I found my way to a popular deli counter offering all manner of salads, sandwiches and desserts. As I gazed at the multitude of choices in front of me, the line became longer and longer behind me while I tried to make up my mind what to eat. The server on the other side of the counter was obviously annoyed with me, so I quickly pointed to a couple of items and went to the check-out. My head was spinning as I found my way back to the office. Even the elevators were a re-learning experience for me. I had used elevators in Johannesburg, but they were nothing like the high speed ones in this building. I felt like I was traveling through outer space! How I was able to perform my duties as a secretary is still a mystery to me. God was surely with me!

A few months after we arrived in Canada, M followed us. We were later divorced, but while we were together in Toronto, he had convinced me to take out a bank loan for him. That loan caused me to have a debt I could not pay. One morning in perhaps 1990, 1991 or 1992 as I was preparing to go to work, I turned on the television. I did not normally do that and I had never heard of the 700 Club. Pat Robertson had a Word of Knowledge and it seemed as though he was looking right at me from the screen saying, "God is going to bring someone to pay that $5,000 debt for you!" That was the amount of my debt!! I thanked the Lord for His Word to me and then I forgot about it.

There is nothing I want more than to have never put my children through such trials and pain by my disobedience to God. I believe that there were times when I had lost my reverential fear of the Lord. I am sure that Abba Father's heart was breaking as He watched me go my own way, ignoring the warning signs He had put in front of me.

Proverbs 19:23 The fear of the LORD leads to life, And he who has it will abide in satisfaction; He will not be visited with evil.

I continue to pray for healing of the emotional wounds that Josie and Carl have suffered because of me. I have come humbly and earnestly in confession and repentance to God and I know personally without a doubt that my God is a God of restoration! When I was in my deepest pit of despair He was there with me. When I cried out to God asking Him if he had forgotten me and my children, He reminded me that He would never leave me or forsake me; that He is closer than a brother; and that when all others would forsake me, He would still be there. Just as in a race to the finish line, when you stumble and fall, you get up and keep going. So it is in this life.

Early on in my walk with the Lord, I heard Kenneth Hagin Sr. on a tape giving the example of running to answer the phone and tripping over the wire and falling on the way to answer it. He said, "You wouldn't just lay there and say, 'Oh well; I fell so now I can't answer the phone.' No! You would get up and answer it!"

My children and I moved several times while living in Toronto due to circumstances in our lives. One cool summer evening while living in a house in the east end of Toronto, my son and I were sitting on the front steps counting all the times that we had moved. I don't remember the number we came up with but it

Chapter 15

was an outrageous amount. Even in our most desperate situations, God always provided for us.

It was while we were living in the east end that I came to know about Kamp Kuriou. It is a Christian camp in Parry Sound, Ontario that was established in 1971 by the Reverend David Bowen and his wife Margaret. They have since gone to be with the Lord and I am thankful to have had the opportunity to spend even a very short time with two such pillars of the faith. Their son, Allan Bowen, who is now the president, is carrying on their vision of helping children.

I felt that the Lord told me to go to the camp one particular week to be a counselor. When Pastor Bowen Sr. spoke to me and found out my age he said, "Are you sure you want to do this? You will be with the children all the time, even sleeping with them in their cabin."

"Oh yes," I replied, "I'm sure." Pastor and Mrs. Bowen kindly drove me there with them from Toronto the first time I went.

The second time I traveled on the camp bus with all the little campers. By the time I arrived, bedraggled and exhausted, I thought perhaps I had not heard from God after all. As I stepped off the bus a young counselor immediately came up to me and said she was so glad I came. She told me they had been praying for God to send someone because they were short of counselors for the girls. She didn't even seem to notice that I was in my forties! I consider it a great privilege to have had the opportunity to volunteer at the camp for even a short while. It was truly life-changing for me to witness the transformation in young people's lives as they received the love of Jesus during their stay.

While working at an office in the Bloor/Sherbourne area of Toronto, I walked into a Christian bookstore on Huntley Street during my lunch hour. I had no knowledge of the television ministry of 100 Huntley Street which is now known as Crossroads. It was started by David Mainse in the 1970's. This store was part of it and I used to browse there often.

One day, as I was purchasing a book, the music playing through the speakers caught my attention. It sounded Israeli or Middle Eastern to me and I commented to the sales clerk that I liked it. She told me that if I enjoyed that kind of music there was a Messianic congregation in Yorkdale called Melech Yisrael where I could hear more of it. I thanked her and decided to visit the place. I had never even known that there was such a thing as a Messianic congregation or what it was. What a blessing they turned out to be. Messianic Rabbi Hans Vanderwerff and his wife Vonnie had been the spiritual leaders at Melech Yisrael since 1979. They have such a heart for the Jewish people. Their two daughters, Mirjam and Evelyn, and granddaughter Signe worshipped the Lord with Davidic dancing in front of the congregation. My heart leapt for joy the first time that I attended. I truly felt at home. They were a tremendous encouragement to me while I was part of that Congregation.

Hans and Vonnie retired from Melech Yisrael in 1992 but continue with their labor of love through "Comfort Ye My People" ministries. May God richly bless them for their steadfast support of the Jewish people and their tireless work to inform and educate the church about the truth of their Jewish roots and God's will for His chosen people.

Baruch Goldstein from Jews for Jesus was appointed as the next Messianic Rabbi for Congregation Melech Yisrael. In 1993, Jonathan Bernis, the founder and Messianic Rabbi of Congregation Shema Yisrael in Rochester, New York, was organizing his first outreach to the Jewish community of St. Petersburg, Russia. This would be accomplished with street outreach and music festivals. It took place in May 1993 and was a tremendous success with more than 13,000 attending and over 3,600 responses to receive Yeshua (Jesus) as Lord.

My son Carl was attending Melech Yisrael with me and he came home one day and told me that Rabbi Baruch had invited the youth to take part in this outreach. It would include the

Chapter 15

participation of Messianic congregations throughout the United States, Canada and Europe. Carl said he was not interested in participating but I felt a strong a desire to be involved. I contacted our Rabbi and asked him if this outreach was just for the youth. He said "If you would like to come, by all means, come." Almost immediately after I said I would go, I was bombarded with thoughts such as:

You are a single mom. (My children were six months away from being twenty-one and twenty-two years old.)

You don't have the money to go.

Don't you remember you once said that you would NEVER go to Russia?

The best one was, *You're not spiritual enough to go on such a mission!*

So, about a week later, I told Baruch, "I'm sorry but I made a mistake. I can't go on this outreach." He asked me why and I said, "Because I am not spiritual enough."

He immediately exclaimed, "Good, then God can use you!" I will always remember Baruch for that statement. The only thing left for me to do was to trust God to provide the funds for my air fare and passport.

I asked Josie and Carl not to let their Aunt Gilda know of my plans to travel to Russia. I felt that she would not understand and would probably attempt to discourage me. I went ahead and made preparations by obtaining a passport, visa, and the necessary immunizations even though I did not yet have the finances for my airfare and accommodations. I knew that if the Lord had called me, He surely would provide. I was employed as an administrative assistant at the Michener Institute in Toronto and had scheduled my vacation time for the ten days of the outreach, which meant I had to work until the day before the trip. One week before departure I was informed that the funds had been provided and my airfare and accommodation had been purchased! The members of our congregation knew who the participants of the outreach were. As far as I know they provided the funds for me. There was one lady in particular, Ruth, who donated the bulk of my financial needs. I will be forever grateful to her for her obedience to the Lord.

The week before my trip, I became ill and could not keep any food in my stomach except for dry soda crackers and flat Coca Cola. I called my doctor and he told me that it sounded like a virus that was going around and it would most likely pass through my system in about ten days. I said, "I don't have ten days!" I was told to be sure to bring my own toilet paper to St. Petersburg because the toilet paper in Russia was brutal. I decided, considering my condition, that I would need a lot of it. There was probably more toilet paper in my suitcase than clothing.

I called Gil that week to tell her about my plans. I wondered why she took it so calmly. During our next phone conversation, she mentioned that she had also visited St. Petersburg, Florida and it was a really nice place. *Oh, oh*, I thought. *I guess I better tell her that it is not in Florida.* "Gil," I said, "I'm going to St. Petersburg, RUSSIA."

"What?" she exclaimed. "Are you crazy?" Now, that sounded more like my sister. Anyway, she finally accepted it.

The night before we were to leave, I sat down on my bed after packing and re-packing my suitcase at least four times. I was not feeling very well. I said, "Lord, I don't know if I can do this tomorrow."

Immediately, I heard that familiar still small voice inside of me saying, "Resist the devil and he will flee from you." That was all I needed to hear.

I said, "Okay, Lord, I'll go."

James 4:7 *Therefore submit to God. Resist the devil and he will flee from you.*

The next morning, Gil surprised me by coming over early to see me off and to give me some U.S. dollars that she had saved

Chapter 15

from one of her vacations. God bless her. She said, "If I know you, you are going to Russia without a penny in your pocket!"

I replied, "Gil, I'm going with a group. I don't need any money." She insisted I take it anyway and was I ever glad, when I got to Russia, that she had given it to me. No one had told me that I needed to buy my own bottled water over there!

Before Gil left, we went to the local grocery store where I bought several granola bars and packages of nuts and raisins in case I had a problem with the food in Russia. It turned out to be a wise decision because other than the imported yogurt and black bread that we were served at the hotel, the food was too oily for my digestion because of having been ill. I had brought so many granola bars with me that I was able to share some with my roommate and to leave a few with the Russian attendants on our floor of the hotel when we left. Of course, that meant I had to re-pack my dilapidated old suitcase one more time!

[Even though my sister and I have had our differences—the biggest one at the time of this writing being not agreeing that Yeshua (Jesus) is our Jewish Messiah—our love for each other is indestructible.]

When our team from Melech Yisrael arrived at JFK airport in New York City, we had to report to a nurse, Camille. She was traveling with the group from Rochester, New York. Camille wanted to know if any of us had need of special medications while in St. Petersburg. She took one look at me and said, "Are you sure you want to travel? You don't look well at all." I think my face was as green as the outfit I was wearing.

What I really wanted to reply was, "You know, you're right, I feel terrible. I think I should fly right back to Toronto." But the words that came out of my mouth were, "Yes, the Lord told me to come and He will heal me as I go."

She replied, "Okay, but be sure to drink plenty of fluids and don't hesitate to come to me if there is anything you need." Camille then gave me some orange juice and I was on my way. Later, in Russia, she saw me on the street and told me that she could hardly recognize me; that I looked so vibrant and healthy compared to how I had appeared at the airport. God is faithful!

While we were still at JFK Airport, I noticed that a tall, blonde, muscular man was helping some of the ladies with their bags. I approached him to see if he might carry my clumsy suitcase for me. I had tied a rope around it in hopes that my belongings would not go flying out, especially the toilet paper! It didn't go too well. He hurriedly replied that he was too busy helping people from his own team and that I would have to find someone else. We eventually boarded the jet and became airborne. While others were walking around meeting each other, I sat back and tried to concentrate on not feeling sick to my stomach. I had just settled in nicely when I noticed someone coming towards my seat.

Oh no! It's that same guy that I asked to carry my suitcase. He's still wearing that baseball cap. He must be an American for sure! I hope he doesn't notice me. I can't believe that I just went up to some man I didn't even know and asked him to carry my bag. I feel so embarrassed. I can't imagine what he must think of me! Sure enough, he came right over to me and introduced himself. "Hi, I'm John!"

Before I could even answer, he began asking me questions in rapid succession. First, my name; where I was from; how old I was; if I had any children; and if I was single. When he said, "I'm looking for a wife," I reached my limit of patience.

"Wait just a minute! If God has a wife for you, you won't have to go around asking all these questions. You will know her when you see her. Anyway, it is better to stay single than to be married to the wrong person."

At that, he quickly made his exit by politely saying, "Nice meeting you."

When Karen, who was travelling with me, returned to her seat next to me, I warned her about him. "See that guy. Watch out for him. He says that he is looking for a wife. Just because a man

Chapter 15

goes on a mission trip and says he is a Christian, it does not mean that he really is one."

We had several hours layover in Finland before continuing on to St. Petersburg and I had never seen so many tall, blonde, fair complexioned people in my life. They were very friendly and accommodating and though tiring, our layover was enjoyable. Next was our arrival in Russia and what an experience that was. In sharp contrast to the airport in Finland, we were met by gruff female attendants who quickly herded us off the plane and onto shuttle buses. They would count, "One, two, three, four and then stop and put out their arm and say, "You go; you stay." When they came to me, they said, "Go." My two young companions, Karen and Michelle, were told to stay which meant they would have to wait for the next shuttle bus.

The girls panicked and grabbed onto me as they sputtered, "We're together. We can't be separated." We finally managed to convince the stern woman to allow us to stay with each other.

When we arrived at the hotel, which was palatial—taking up a whole city block, we were organized into our groups and paired up with our roommates. My roommate was a young woman from New York City. We made our way through the massive dimly lit hallways until we came to our room. I am glad to say that, unlike some of the others, we had no bedbugs. However, the mosquitoes were ferocious at night. I took to sleeping with a small towel over my face because there were no screens on the windows, and it was so hot that we had to leave them open for air. It was during the season of "White Nights." It did not get dark until past midnight and the streets were teeming with activity. We were instructed to leave our room keys with matrons that sat at a desk in the hallway. Our passports and any important belongings were kept for us in a safe place by the United States leadership of the mission.

Our schedule was pretty full. We met outside to go to breakfast at 6 a.m. We had to meet outside because the only way to get to the dining room was from the street. After breakfast, we were taken to different areas of the city to distribute flyers that had information in Russian about the evening festivals. There was also a Russian interpreter with each team in case we had opportunity to speak or pray with people.

Each day, after the evening meal, we attended the festivals and that was where I met up with John again. We were instructed to be "gummy bears" which meant that we were to attach ourselves to the "anti missionaries" who were trying to stop the Jewish people from coming into the auditorium. These "anti missionaries" were religious Jews who had heard about the outreach and wanted to prevent other Jews from hearing about Yeshua, their Jewish Messiah. Some had even been sent over from America. So, we were to stick to them like glue to distract them so they could not harass those who wanted to come inside. I noticed that John seemed to be really good at this. He was engaging several of them in conversation and was talking circles around them. I thought to myself that it would really be fun to tag along with him to perhaps learn a thing or two. Before I knew it, everyone had entered the building and it was time for us to go in too.

The evening festivals were dynamic and life changing. The members of the dance troupe leaped and spun with vigor to the melodious tunes of Jewish folk music that flowed through the auditorium like rivers of living water. The Spirit-filled worship to almighty God drove out the spiritual forces that would attempt to hold the people back from hearing about their Messiah. The Lord's salvation message delivered each night by the speakers was deeply affecting, piercing the heart. I was overjoyed to see so many of these beautiful Russians, many of them my Jewish people, rushing to the front with tears streaming down their faces to surrender their lives to Yeshua.

The following is a quote from Sid Roth, a Jewish Believer in Jesus, who hosts the television show "It's Supernatural." "After the Soviet Union crumbled, I accompanied my friend Jonathan Bernis on his first Jewish evangelistic outreach trip to St. Peters-

Chapter 15

burg, Russia. We both were ecstatic to see thousands of Jewish people running to the altars to be saved. This was the first time in 2,000 years such a large number of Jewish people had come to their Messiah."

One evening while waiting to pray for people, I asked one of my interpreters, a young Christian man named Peter, how it was for him under Communism. He told me, "We thought we had a good life. We were told that everyone in America was poor. It was a surprise to us when we found out that it wasn't true."

I learned two Russian words, pajolasta (please) and spaseba (thank you) which I used at every opportunity. The two interpreters that were assigned to the team I was on were Peter, whom I have mentioned already, and a young Christian girl, Nadia. I kept in contact with the two of them for a time after I got back to North America, but mailing letters or packages was complicated and we finally lost touch.

One day I wandered off by myself on a side street that looked like an open flea market. I began distributing flyers and praying for people. Suddenly Peter appeared and grabbed my arm, hurrying me out to the main boulevard. "Peter," I said, "Why did you pull me out of there?"

"Don't you know?" he replied, "This is the Russian black market and you were in great danger there. Don't go anywhere by yourself. Promise me!"

"Peter," I answered, "those people need Jesus too and, in any case, I have angels watching over me." But, I did as he asked since he seemed to be so concerned.

I had a harrowing experience on a trolley car in St. Petersburg. A few of the girls, along with one of our interpreters, decided to go for a ride. We had to purchase our tickets at a kiosk on the street which were to be deposited into a receptacle in the middle of the trolley car. Everyone just piled in the front and center doors. There was seemingly no order to it. Someone pushed me onto the car through the middle door so I wouldn't be separated from my group. I found myself hanging on for dear life, pressed against the car door inside while praying that it would not accidentally open. There were so many people in front of me that I couldn't even move as we sped through the streets at a maddening pace!

It reminded me of the incident when I was a young girl on the Scrambler ride with Gil, and our friends, Pat and Joanne, at the Canadian National Exhibition (CNE) in Toronto. I was lost in daydreaming about how the Scrambler safety bar wasn't locked when suddenly, the trolley stopped and I almost fell out onto the pavement as I joined my friends. I still had my ticket in my hand because I was not able to get through to the receptacle to deposit it.

John was brave enough to go on the underground subway. He later told me that it was fascinating how the escalator reached deep into the bowels of the earth and moved so speedily. When you came up it felt like you had been shot out of a cannon. Perhaps that was why everyone seemed to be rushing so quickly past us when we stood at the subway exits to give out tracts! It was as if the people were being propelled by some invisible force onto the street!

One night during the festival my interpreter, Peter, told me that he had a heart condition, so I asked John to pray for him. He was visibly touched by the Lord and said that he believed he was healed. During the altar calls, after praying for some of the women, they would embrace me and ask for my address in Canada so they could write to me. Once, a man asked for my address and after I gave it to him I thought, "What have I done!" The next day I mentioned it to one of my team members and John overheard. He immediately gave me a lecture about how a woman alone in a strange land should, under no circumstances, give out her address.

That same morning, I had been eating breakfast in the dining hall when John came by to fill up an extra tray with food. I must have been staring at him because he told me rather sheepishly that it was for his roommate, Jim. I guess John did not want me to

Chapter 15

think he was being greedy, which was the furthest thing from my mind. I was just curious why he would be filling up a tray with food and not sitting down to eat it with the rest of us. Apparently, Jim had broken his ankle while participating in the Israeli folk dancing during the festival the previous night. He was laid up in his room with ice packs on his ankle which by this time had turned green. No one, including Jim, wanted him to end up in a Russian hospital so he spent the last two days of the mission as a prayer warrior. The Lord supernaturally strengthened Jim as he hobbled around on one leg because he was not able to obtain crutches without going to a hospital for treatment. During the two days that he was incapacitated, a few of the Russian people he had met on the streets came to visit him. It happened that one was a nurse and she also advised that he wait until he returned to the United States to see a doctor. Thankfully, Jim was finally able to access the much needed crutches at the airport on our flight home. Jim Appel is now Rabbi Jim of Congregation Shema Yisrael in Rochester, New York.

One morning while we were assembling our teams on the street, I saw John taking pictures with his Kodak camera. He worked at Eastman Kodak in Rochester, New York. We began calling him "Mr. Kodak" because he was always snapping photos of everything and everybody. I said to him, "Gee, I wish I had a camera so I could take some pictures home to show my children."

"Well," he replied. "If you give me your address in Toronto, I will send some to you."

I promptly answered as I placed my hands on my hips, "I thought you said that a woman traveling on her own in a strange land should never give out her address!"

He said with a twinkle in his eye, "Take your chances, Lady." His friend Eli raised his eyebrows and grinned at John while John grinned back at him as if he had just won a contest.

I thought their camaraderie was cute as I replied, "Okay then, I WILL take my chances." On the final day of our mission, the leadership had arranged for us to go on tour buses to see a few sights in St. Petersburg before we returned home. What stood out to me about the city were its wide boulevards, contrasted by its winding alleys dotted with gift kiosks selling chocolates and all manner of items. The intricate architectural design of the buildings was magnificent to behold. Rather than high rises, the structures appeared to be two or three stories high, stretching over long distances. Our hotel occupied a whole city block. We saw the church that was built where Emperor Alexander II was assassinated in 1881. It was a typical Russian style church with onion domes and a glorious multitude of colors that glistened in the sunlight. We beheld the magnificent beauty of the Neva River while traveling across the Palace Bridge to visit the elaborate Palace Square.

Whenever I boarded a bus, John was already inside at the front. He would say to me, "There's a seat here, if you like." For the life of me, I could not figure out how he always managed to be the first one on the bus. On one of our stops, I purchased some Russian and Swiss chocolate to take home to Josie and Carl. I shared one of the bars with John and he asked with animated interest and enthusiasm, "Where did you find that chocolate?" I had no idea that he had an absolute passion for chocolate!

While riding the bus, we would make small talk and in my mind I would be thinking, *What can I say to this man? He is so spiritual. Everything I say will sound so stupid.* I later found out from John that he was thinking to himself at the same time, *What can I say to her. She is from the city and is so sophisticated. I am just a country boy. Everything I say will sound so stupid!*

It was finally time to leave Russia and fly back to North America. My heart was breaking as we said goodbye to our interpreters. I will never forget the Russian people that I met on that trip. They were so open, giving, loving, and resilient. I felt right at home amongst them.

Chapter 15

On the return flight, I was placed in the middle of a long row which I found to be extremely uncomfortable, especially when I wanted to get up to visit the ladies' room. I had to crawl over so many bodies to get to the aisle. I saw an opening up ahead and even though it was not with our group, I headed for it so I could have some breathing space. I sat down and for a while it was fine until the people around me started to get drunk and rowdy. After talking about Jesus with those closest to me, I decided to return to my previous seat. As I was walking back, I heard a familiar voice say, "There's a seat here, if you like." I kid you not! John had an aisle seat and the window seat beside him was empty. I was not about to pass up an offer like that. I climbed onto my window seat and settled in for the rest of the trip.

A movie was playing for the passengers. It was "Honey, I Shrunk The Kids" and John's eyes were glued to it. I was shocked. Why, I thought this spiritual man would have been praying twenty-four hours a day and instead, he was enjoying a movie.

The movie finished and between moments of trying to catch some much needed sleep, we chatted a little. Even though we knew very little about each other, we had the common bond as a brother and sister in the Lord and we shared our impressions of Russia during our short stay there.

John began to talk to me about his father. He told me how he and his dad had planted hundreds of trees on their property in Fredonia. I thought this revealed a very special and tender side to his personality. He said his dad died in 1990, which was only a few years before this trip. As he was reminiscing about the trees, I could see that he really loved and missed his father. He told me that when he worked in Rochester, New York he used to drive to Fredonia almost every weekend to spend time with his dad. I do not remember the words I spoke to him during this tender moment, but it really moved him. He clamped his huge hand on top of mine and said with tears in his eyes, "You were sent from God to tell me that." Instead of giving thanks to God for giving me words that John needed to hear, all I could think of was that my pastor was sitting directly behind us and what would he think if he saw me holding hands with this man!

We settled in for the rest of the flight, enjoying each other's company. We didn't need a lot of words or conversation. My eyelids soon became heavy with sleep and before I knew it we had arrived at JFK airport in New York City. There was a short bus ride to board the planes that would take us to our separate destinations. We said our goodbyes and I wondered if I would ever see John again.

A few weeks after arriving home from Russia, I called John to see if he was going to send me the pictures he had promised. He promptly sent me the photos and that phone call was the beginning of a long distance telephone relationship. I had not yet told any of my fellow employees at the office about meeting John. To my surprise, a short while after we had been communicating by telephone I was summoned to the reception area of the educational institute where I worked as an administrative assistant. On the counter was a beautiful bouquet of red roses and a card from John. I was thrilled by this romantic gesture and, of course, the ladies in the office wanted to know all about my secret romance, now no longer a secret.

After communicating by phone for several weeks, we decided that I should visit John in the United States. I boarded a bus in Toronto that took me to Buffalo where he was to pick me up. I was a nervous wreck! I kept thinking, *Here I am, forty-seven years old and going on a weekend date. I can't do this.*

It was raining when I arrived and John showed up with a huge umbrella. Like a true gentleman, he carried my small bag and shielded me from the rain. We drove to Rochester, New York, where he took me to Cobbs Hill which was a park he particularly liked. We went for a stroll on the wet grass and started to climb up a slight incline. I was not wearing the correct shoes for this type of walking and I began sliding backwards. John immediately

Chapter 15

held his arm behind my back to keep me from falling. His arm felt so strong and secure as I leaned into it. Coming to my senses, I said, "I think we should take the long way to the top of the hill and walk on the concrete path."

Afterwards, we drove to Kim's apartment where I would be spending the night. Kim is a sweet sister in the Lord who was attending Shema Yisrael at that time. I appreciated her kind gesture to give us dinner and accommodate me during my stay. The three of us went to the Friday night Shabbat service where I was introduced to the congregation.

John had arranged for me to stay at the White Inn in Fredonia for Saturday night. I was so tense that I had a splitting headache the whole weekend. He had ordered a beautiful bouquet of roses for my room at the Inn. I remember thinking, as I lay down to have a nap before he was to pick me up for dinner: *If I didn't have this horrible headache, I could really enjoy myself.*

John arrived and as we were leaving the Inn, a beautiful wedding ceremony was taking place on the front lawn. It really added a touch of romance to our evening, although with a pounding headache, I didn't feel very romantic at all. We drove to the Chautauqua Institute where we had a lovely stroll through the grounds on our way to the grandiose historic Athenaeum Hotel. John had made reservations for dinner on the patio as it was a perfect early summer evening to eat outdoors.

Once again, I was wearing ridiculous shoes for walking. My feet were aching and my head was throbbing but I soldiered on! What did we behold as we walked toward the patio? Another outdoor wedding ceremony! This was beginning to look like a set-up.

After dinner, on the way back to Fredonia, John took me to meet his sister, Rita. Rita very graciously made us delicious cool drinks to sip on the back deck of her country home where we watched fireflies dancing long into the night. By this time, my headache had subsided somewhat and I was beginning to feel a little more relaxed.

The next morning, which was Sunday, John picked me up at the White Inn to drive me to the bus station in Buffalo. On the way there, he said, "God has shown me that you are to be my wife." I pondered this in my heart. John knew all about my past. I hadn't kept anything from him. Could it be possible that God would be granting me this new beginning?

While my American Knight in Shining Armor was courting me, he told me a little more about himself. John was born in 1946 and grew up in Fredonia, New York. He had an older brother, Larry, and a younger sister, Rita. His mother was of Polish descent and his father's family was from the New England States. There were about seven years between John and his brother and another seven years between him and his sister.

During his earliest childhood years, his family resided in an old gas station garage that had been converted into living quarters. When John rode the school bus home, he would often get off a stop ahead, so the children would not know where he lived. Speaking of school, John felt that it was an unnecessary diversion in his life. He much preferred to romp and explore through the woods and grape vineyards with his dog, Muffin, and fly kites in the fields. He developed make-believe friends or thought perhaps angels were keeping him company while he enjoyed God's creation. The family did possess a television and, as my sister and I did, he enjoyed the Howdy Doody show and watched the test patterns.

Sometime around 1956, John's parents moved their little family to a country environment at the edge of town on the Fredonia/Stockton Road. That was where he had planted all the trees with his dad. They lived in an old farm house and raised a few chickens. One of John's chores was to gather, cut, split, and stack wood for their wood burning stove which, of course, was Muffin's favorite spot during the winter months. This lively Britney Spaniel would curl up on the circular rope mat in front of the stove to get cozy and warm while the icicles melted off of his fur after romp-

Chapter 15

ing in snow piles outside while John was shoveling a path from the house to the road. Later, he would climb into bed with John, adding much appreciated warmth for the night.

He spent his summers playing with friends a few miles away across fields and through the woods. As a teenager, he would walk or jog along the dirt roads, taking in the fragrance of wild flowers and peppermint that were growing in the ditches. Muffin would run ahead chasing butterflies as they headed toward the creek for some new adventure or a dip in a swimming hole that the rain storm had carved out the night before. Before returning home, he would find a spot on the hill and lay back to watch the clouds float by while Muffin would stalk and chase his prey. On those hot summer days, John would be absorbed in the earthy environment, enveloped with a sense of God being with him. His biggest concern back then was whether there would be a haying job for the next day or an opportunity to pick berries for some extra cash.

Little did he realize, growing up, that all of this was God's preparation and equipping for the rapidly approaching events that were on the horizon. He went on to graduate in 1964 from Fredonia High School and, in 1965 he was drafted into the United States Army and sent to Viet Nam.

Amazingly, God miraculously spared John's life more than once. One time was on a Friday evening in the 1980's when he was returning to Fredonia from Rochester on his BMW motorcycle, traveling along Route 20 through the Orchard park area. He came to a very busy intersection around 6 p.m. The light turned green and he zoomed forward when suddenly a car cut directly in front of him causing his bike to T-bone the back passenger door. He flew into the air over the car in a 180 degree turn and landed in the other lane where thankfully there was no traffic. He did not lose consciousness and felt as if God's hand, or an angel, had gently set him down on the ground. He didn't skid on the pavement and even his brand new Bell helmet was not chipped.

He was so happy to be alive and not hurt that he didn't pay

any attention to the driver of the car who had caused the accident. Two men from his original lane of traffic came over. They had a truck and took him and his bike, which was a little bent, back to Fredonia. Glory to God, the next morning he was a little stiff but suffered no injuries. Later, he traded that 750 cc bike for a nice red 900 cc BMW.

John loved to ride like the wind on his new red BMW motorcycle. He used it to travel from Rochester to New Mexico with his buddy Terry. He also rode to Texas to spend time with his sister Rita or to Florida to visit with his Aunt Wanda. But it was on one of his weekend trips back home to Fredonia to visit his dad and his brother Larry that the following miracle took place.

John said to me "I will never forget what happened on a rainy, late spring morning in Rochester, N.Y. in 1980. I loved my 900 cc BMW motorcycle which had taken me on some great rides to New Mexico, Colorado and Florida. That morning, it was raining and I jumped on the expressway completely unaware that about a mile down the road was a minor accident and traffic was slowing down. I was three lanes over in the express lane doing around 55-60 mph when things got really slow in front of me. I will tell you this; bikes, brakes, and rain do not mix well. I was in big trouble. My last thought before temporarily losing consciousness was, *If I make it to the pavement all these cars will run over me!*

"The bike went down to the left and I flew to the right. When I came to, a van's left rear wheel was on my knee. As I pounded on the van, the driver seemed to be more in shock than I was and he pulled forward to free me. The medics who were at the previous accident were alerted to my plight and rushed over. The police later told me that there was a six car pileup because of people trying to avoid hitting me as I lay there. I knew I was hurt badly as every breath brought excruciating pain.

"Later, at Strong Memorial Hospital, I learned that I had suffered a collapsed lung and two fractured ribs from hitting the side of the van. Amazingly, I suffered no injury to my leg or knee that

Chapter 15

the van tire was sitting on! Once again, God's hand saved me. The miracle was that five days later, I walked out of the hospital and went hiking!

"The other miracle was that a very good friend of mine came to believe in Jesus after hearing all the details of my accident. I told God that surely there could have been an easier way to have witnessed to him."

I was beginning to see that John and I had a lot in common as God had supernaturally spared both our lives.

I made another visit to Fredonia where I met John's brother Larry and Larry's wife Barb. They made me feel like part of the family right away and Barb was one of the most amazing, old fashioned country cooks that I have ever known. (Barb has since gone to be with the Lord.)

John visited me several times in Toronto where he stayed in a hotel a short distance from my apartment at Finch and Dufferin Streets. During those visits he attended Congregation Melech Yisrael with me so that everyone got to know him.

On one of his visits, he showed up carrying a small, white plastic bag and asked if we could go for a walk. "What's in the bag?" I asked.

"It's my camera. I don't want any dust to get into it." As we were walking I was thinking this was a strange explanation because we were not walking on the beach and I had never seen anyone wrap their camera in a plastic bag like that before. We were at a busy intersection close to my home, heading towards the park on the other side.

Suddenly, John exclaimed with urgency, "We have to get to that park bench right away or my heart is going to burst!"

Oh no, I thought. *He's going to have a heart attack right here in the traffic!*

As soon as the traffic light turned green, we scurried across the road, making our way to the empty park bench. When we sat down, John nervously unwrapped the little package he had been clutching so carefully as he said, "I can't wait any longer." To my astonishment, it was a little jewelry box, which he opened to reveal a glistening diamond ring! Then I heard his gentle voice asking me the glorious question, "Will you marry me?"

I was stunned. It must have seemed like an eternity to him until I finally uttered, "Yes, yes, I will marry you." That was in August, 1993.

In the short time that I had become acquainted with John, I came to know that he was a man of prayer and a man after God's own heart. I never felt intimidated by him as with other men in the past. I suddenly became overwhelmed with the prospect of getting married again. "How am I going to tell the children? They hardly know you. How am I going to tell my family? You haven't even met my sister and my brothers yet."

John said calmly (being calm now after he had finally popped the question), "Let's pray." We prayed and put everything into God's hands.

"Is there anywhere around here that we can get something to eat?" he asked.

"Well, do you like chicken?"

"Sure!"

"The Swiss Chalet is just up the street. Let's go there. They have really good barbecued chicken," I said as I was thinking, *If Gilda knew we were going for chicken she would say to me, "Don't you ever order anything else besides chicken when you go out to eat?"*

While we were enjoying our meal we told each other about the thoughts we had while riding on the bus in St. Petersburg. "I can't believe I thought you were so spiritual that I couldn't even talk to you!" I told John.

"Hey, you're not as sophisticated as I thought you were either," he replied with a silly grin on his face.

"Would you prefer that I was one of those really sophisticated city girls?"

Chapter 15

"No, not at all. I feel much more comfortable with you just the way you are."

"Now that you're comfortable with me, I might as well tell you that I was really shocked on the plane when you told me you were looking for a wife. I'm glad that the Lord arranged our circumstances to keep meeting up with each other because I really didn't want to have anything to do with you after that. Why DID you say such a thing to a woman you didn't even know?"

"Ron," he began. (He called me 'Ron' right from the beginning of our relationship.) "In Rochester, I had been attending a class on prayer at Bethel Full Gospel Church. All of us in the class had been praying for each other and my prayer had been for God to give me a wife. By the way, after we are married I'm going to take you to meet them. Anyhow, when I knew that I was going on the outreach to Russia, I shared that I had always found it really difficult to communicate with other people, especially having a conversation with someone I didn't know. The prayer group all prayed for God to give me confidence and boldness. Also, someone had a word for me that something great was going to happen to me while in Russia. When I noticed you in your seat on the plane, I felt bad that I had been so gruff with you at the airport in New York. I was really coming over to apologize. I don't know what happened but all of a sudden I felt such confidence and all my questions just came pouring out of me. Looks like God answered my prayer! "

"Oh boy," I said, "I need to tell you that I warned Karen about you. I told her you might not even be a Christian!" I almost choked on my food as I started to laugh so hard trying to finish my sentence.

John laughed. "I guess Karen is in for a big surprise when we announce our engagement at the congregation on Saturday."

"By the way, there's one more thing," I said.

"What now?"

"Well, when you said your heart was going to burst before you gave me the engagement ring this afternoon, I thought you were literally going to have a heart attack!"

"Ya know, Ron, you really are God's gift to me."

The following Saturday, when our engagement was announced at Melech Yisrael, Karen couldn't believe her ears! She congratulated us, and we laughed so hard that tears came to our eyes!

After the Saturday service, John and I reminisced about our adventures in St. Petersburg. I told him about how much I liked the German restaurant where Karen and I ate one night.

"Once I found out about that place, I ate there every night!" John said.

"WHAT?! Too bad I didn't know you so well then. You could have bought me a few meals, too. I didn't have any extra money and what I mostly ate in Russia were my granola bars and yogurt that was imported from Finland."

John answered, "Hey, you're kidding. That's all I ate too, the yogurt, I mean. If I had known you had all those granola bars with you, I would have helped you eat them! Ya know, it IS too bad we hadn't become friendly earlier in the mission because I usually went to the German restaurant alone. I would have really enjoyed your company."

Sometime later, after letting Josie and Carl know about our plans, we had a get-together for my family at Stan's house. I can't say that it was entirely without some tension but at least everyone now knew that John and I were officially engaged.

After John returned to Rochester, we continued our telephone relationship between his visits to me in Toronto until we were married. During one of those conversations, I told John about my $5,000 debt and that I did not feel we could set a wedding date until such time as I had paid it. He immediately said he would take care of it. I was astonished and I declared that there was no way that I could allow him to do such a thing. He insisted and then I remembered the Word from God for me on the 700 Club that I had actually forgotten about. I told John about it and

Chapter 15

he said, "Praise the Lord. Then, it's settled!" God is so faithful.

Shortly after John had proposed to me, I took him to visit the Toronto Airport Christian Fellowship (now called "Catch the Fire Toronto"). I had been invited to this church a couple of years before I met John when it was part of the Vineyard churches. In any case, we attended a "Meet the Pastor" lunch after the service where I asked Pastor Arnott to pray for us because I needed to be sure that it was God's will for me to be married. Afterwards, Pastor Arnott brought a gentleman over. He said, "I hope you two don't mind but this man says he has a word for you from the Lord." The gentleman did not know anything about us or even that we were engaged. He told us that God was going to use us as iron sharpens iron to chip away all the rough edges from each other. That prophetic word came to pass. I had been a single mother making all the decisions on my own and John had never been married before. We were both strong-willed and it has been a glorious experience as God has been molding us together as One New Man in Him.

Ephesians 2: 11-18 Therefore remember that you, once Gentiles in the flesh—who are called Uncircumcision by what is called the Circumcision made in the flesh by hands; that at that time you were without Christ, being aliens from the commonwealth of Israel and strangers from the covenants of promise, having no hope and without God in the world. But now in Christ Jesus you who once were far off have been brought near by the blood of Christ.

For He Himself is our peace, who has made both one, and has broken down the middle wall of separation, having abolished in His flesh the enmity, that is, the law of commandments contained in ordinances, so as to create in Himself one new man from the two, thus making peace, and that He might reconcile them both to God in one body through the cross, thereby putting to death the enmity. And He came and preached peace to you who were afar off and to those who were near. For through Him we both have access by one Spirit to the Father.

It is interesting that for about one year before I had met John, I found myself cherishing every moment I had with my son and daughter because I was sensing that sometime in the near future we would not be living together. It was a perfectly logical thought since they were adults now, but I thought that they would be the ones leaving home, not me!

We set our wedding date for October 3, 1993. I had a vision in my mind of what I wanted my wedding dress to look like and I even drew a picture of it. I searched all over the bridal district on Spadina Avenue because that was where everyone said I should look for my dress. I did not see anything close to resembling it.

I decided to make one more attempt by going to the Eaton's Center on Dundas Street. There it was, on the third floor in a shop called "Yofi" which is a Hebrew word meaning "The beauty of God." I saw the dress in the window and was overwhelmed. It was just as I had envisioned. It was one of a kind as this was a specialty store. I tried it on and it fit me as if it was made for me. It was off-white, vintage, antique Victorian style with delicate lace bodice, short collar with soft puffs on the shoulders and lace cuffs on the sleeves. I felt like a princess as the sales ladies asked me to turn around. The only regret I have is that I asked them to shorten it to the top of my ankles because I did not want it to look too much like a gown since this was not my first marriage. They tried to dissuade me but, in the end, reluctantly shortened it for me. This was only one week before my wedding!

We had a Messianic Jewish wedding and I am forever thankful to the ladies of Congregation Melech Yisrael for all they did for us to make our day such a special and joyous occasion. Two ladies from Melech Yisrael blessed us by baking an elegant wedding cake. Several brothers and sisters in the Lord from Congregation Shema Yisrael in Rochester celebrated with us. My sister and two brothers attended along with John's brother, sister-in law, sister, aunt, and a few of his closest friends from Fredonia, New York.

John's brother Larry was his best man. My son Carl wrote and sang a special song for us and my beautiful daughter Josie was my one and only bridesmaid and, as she was an aspiring photographer, took some of the photos for us.

Of course, our wedding would not have been complete without the traditional Hora, or Chair Dance. We were lifted up onto folding chairs, the exuberant crowd ignoring our feeble protests as we both hung on for dear life! Everyone was dancing and laughing and singing so loudly that they could not hear me frantically screaming that we were sliding off of our chairs. We were very glad to have our feet on solid ground when it was finally over—happy to be alive to delight in the memory!

John was about to experience unexpected tragedy. On our wedding night, before we left Toronto, his older brother suffered a heart attack in his hotel room. I had previously told Carl that we were going to stay the night in Toronto before leaving for our honeymoon at Lake Placid but I had forgotten to tell him which hotel. My son went through the yellow pages of our phone book and found where I had circled a hotel. Thankfully, he tracked us down and gave the phone number to John's sister, Rita, who had called Carl to see if he could find us. We were contacted and spent the night at the hospital with Larry's wife Barb and his sister Rita. John's Aunt Wanda had already flown back to Florida. Larry passed away a few days later and we remained in Toronto to work out all the details involved in such matters. During that time, Mrs. Freedman, my landlady, showed such kindness by cooking food and bringing it to my apartment which she made available to us for the duration of our stay. Dear Mrs. Freedman and her husband were holocaust survivors and it was an honor to have known them.

Of course, we cancelled our Honeymoon and now that all the arrangements surrounding Larry's untimely death had been completed, it was time for John and me to journey to Rochester, New York. My heart was torn between joy and pain. The joy of being joined in marriage to the man whom God had supernaturally brought into my life was contrasted by the emotional, motherly pain of knowing that I would be leaving my children in Canada to live in Rochester, New York. I was only going to be a few hours' drive away but it might as well have been to the other side of the world. Even though Josie and Carl were adults, this would be the first time in twenty-two years that I would be moving to another country and not taking them with me. I struggled with that for a long time. I had said to the Lord; "This can't be of you. You would never ask me to separate from my children." Father God reminded me that I had presented my children to Him when they were little and that I was now to trust Him as their Heavenly Father. When I felt that I could not bear the pain of separation, He reminded me of this verse, My grace is sufficient for you (2 Corinthians 12:9).

My heart was also breaking for my Josie and Carl. I knew it was difficult for them to see me being married again, especially knowing that I would be moving away. They were so gracious and supportive of me during a time when they could have chosen to be angry. If anyone deserves God's blessing over their lives, it is my children.

God has given me over and above what I asked for when I prayed for Him to let me live so my children would not be without a mother. I am still here and my children are not only grown but I have now been blessed with grandchildren. Carl and Josie have been the delight of my life, and I consider it a privilege to have watched them grow up to be the fine man and woman they are today. I have said that every age of my children has been the best age. When they were infants, I thought nothing could be more angelic and when they were toddlers it was fascinating to witness their individual personalities develop. There were times when Josie and Carl were three and four years old when I would stand outside of the room where they were playing just to listen to them as they delightfully chattered away to each other. It boggled my mind that they found so much to say to each other. I am so proud of them as they are a constant joy and encouragement to me, and I stand in awe at the two amazing people that they have become.

Chapter 15

As much as I love them, God loves them with a love that surpasses all human understanding. He has tenderly watched over them all these years and His purpose will surely be fulfilled in their lives. Josie has a heart that loves the unlovable and the Lord has gifted her as a photographer. Carl is a true peacemaker and the Lord has gifted him as a musician. I pray that Josie and Carl's gifts will be used for the glory of God.

Psalm 68:4-5 *Sing to God, sing praises to His name; Extol Him who rides on the clouds, By His name YAH, And rejoice before Him. A father of the fatherless, a defender of widows, is God in His Holy Habitation.*

For My Daughter, Josie

Daughter, my daughter
Where did it start?
When did you become a grown up
And I become a child in your eyes?
I remember walking hand in hand
When you had so many questions
That I thought I couldn't find answers for them all
There never seemed to be an end to our conversations
Or our hugs and kisses and fascinations
Now our times together are quiet
You take my hand when we cross the street
And try to tell me what I should eat
I am so proud of the person you are
Hoping that you know it
I watch you with your children
And the confidence you have
In being a mother
It comes so naturally to you
You are a special gift my lovely one
And I treasure every moment I have with you
Though we cram so much into it
Not knowing when we will be together again
There is a bond between mother and daughter
That distance cannot separate
So, live your life to the fullest
Cherish every moment
And know
That my love for you is forever

# Chapter 15

For My Son, Carl

My son, my son
Don't you know
There's nothing you could ever do
To take away my love for you
I've watched you stumble
I've watched you fall
My heart was breaking through it all
You've overcome against all odds
And I'm so proud of who you are
Your gentle spirit is full of strength
Adversity won't have its way
Over the man you are today
Your tomorrows are written
For you to walk through
There's nothing more for me to do
But stand amazed
And watch you fly on eagles' wings
To greater heights than you have dreamed

CHAPTER 16

"Don't Drop The Cookies!"

And so it came to pass that we began our new life in Rochester, New York. For the first few years of our marriage, October 3rd was an especially difficult time for John as it was our anniversary and the week his only brother died. One of the first things that he did was to take me to the prayer class he had been attending to show everyone in person the answer to their prayers for a wife for him! Needless to say, I was quite a celebrity and, hopefully, an encouragement to others to continue to press in to the Lord to seek the answer to their prayers.

Shortly after we became husband and wife, I took John to Toronto to meet the dear mother of my childhood friends, Pat and Joanne. I knew her now as Nellie. She was once again a widow as she outlived her second husband. Nellie had treated my sister and I as daughters just the same as my mother had treated her girls as daughters. I had invited her to our wedding but she was unable to attend. When I introduced John to her, it was almost as if I was introducing him to my mother. She lovingly and affectionately surprised us by handing us an envelope with a nice sum of money in it. I was taken aback. I had not expected it and it moved me to tears. Nellie attended the Ukrainian Orthodox Church, and I do believe she had a relationship with Jesus. She has since gone to be with the Lord.

After we had been married about three months I received a call from my friend Marjatta in Toronto. Before I met John, I had taken her to a meeting at the Vineyard Church when they were meeting in a small building near the Airport. "Rhonda," she said. "You and John have to come to Toronto and see what is going on here. We are having revival!"

Chapter 16

"Wow, what is happening?"

"Well, we are having such a great time. Laughter is breaking out and we are just enjoying the Presence of the Lord. You have to come," was her emphatic response.

Now, I was thinking *Oh dear, what have I done. Why did I take Marjatta to that church! She is so vulnerable.* What my friend described to me did not fit neatly into my past experience with the Presence of God. (I was the last person that I would have thought would be skeptical of a move of God since I felt that I was really open to the Holy Spirit.)

A few weeks later, we were visiting Melech Yisrael Congregation in Toronto and a couple of good friends, Louis and Nicole, also told us to go to the Vineyard to check it out. They said they felt that God was really moving there in a powerful way. Since Louis and Nicole were two people that I felt were spiritually mature and discerning, we decided to go to the Vineyard and see for ourselves. This was in the early days of what became known as the "Toronto Blessing."

When we arrived, the small facility was packed to overflowing. As we entered, I said to John, "Either I am feeling ill or God is touching me." I felt a tremendous heat in my body during the whole service. There were others who were laughing or jerking or falling on the floor. I had no doubt that I was personally experiencing the Presence of the Lord even though some of the manifestations I was seeing were different than what I personally had witnessed before.

By the time we were able to visit again, the church was meeting in a larger facility on Atwell Drive. I had been desperate to go again because John and I had been praying and doing spiritual warfare about the anxiety disorder I was afflicted with, and I just wanted to be free. There had been times when I would be in a church service in Rochester and silently saying to Jesus, "When am I going to be able to sit here like everyone else and not be going through a spiritual battle in my mind at the same time?" The more I tried to control it, the worse it would seem to get.

One time, while working at a law office in Rochester, I went to lunch with one of my co-workers who I was witnessing to about Jesus. We were in a cafeteria setting and, suddenly, as I lifted my cup to my lips, my neck twitched and I had to replace my coffee to the table. I immediately broke out in a cold sweat as fear swept over me like a suffocating wet blanket. I quickly told her that I was sorry, but I was not feeling well and had to leave. *Now*, I thought, *it's so bad that I can't even go out to lunch with a friend or tell anyone about what Jesus has done for me. What are they going to think when they see such a wreck of a person in front of them?* I cried out to God in my heart all the way back to the office. "Please help me. I don't know what to do!"

John was the first person I ever told about these anxiety attacks. He has been the only person in my life that I have felt I could totally trust with my innermost feelings and know that he will support me and pray for me.

We drove to the church in Toronto again and as we entered the new building, I felt the tangible Presence of God once more. This time I had such a peace and when it was time for prayer, I was powerfully touched by the Lord and as I got up from the floor, I knew I was free! No one can tell me that what happened was not of God. The devil does not set you free the way Jesus set me free that night! That was in 1994. It is now 2012 and I am still free. Praise the Lord! As a matter of fact, John and I recently went on a tour of a lighthouse in Dunkirk, New York, and I know that I never could have gone up the steps to the tower and stand on the lookout ledge if I had not had that encounter with the Power of God. In the past I would have been paralyzed with fear because the stairs were steep and winding and you could see through them as we were suspended in the air, so to speak. John and I are thankful for the faithfulness to God and obedience to the Holy Spirit of John and Carol Arnott and all of their ministry team and staff at Catch the Fire Toronto (formerly Toronto Airport Christian Fel-

Chapter 16

lowship). Many times since I experienced deliverance from those anxiety attacks, I have been in a church service and thanked Jesus for the freedom He has given me.

John 8:36 *Therefore if the Son makes you free, you shall be free indeed.*

Revelation 12:11 *And they overcame him by the blood of the Lamb and by the word of their testimony, and they did not love their lives to the death.*

We attended whenever we could over the next several years and John had the privilege of participating as a "catcher" during prayer on many occasions and was powerfully touched by God during those meetings.

One evening when I was resting in the Presence of the Lord, I had a vision of Jesus standing before me and taking a white robe and placing it over me as He said, "I have always seen you this way."

1 Samuel 16:7 *But the LORD said to Samuel, Do not look at his appearance or at his physical stature, because I have refused him. For the LORD does not see as man sees; for man looks at the outward appearance, but the LORD looks at the heart.*

He reminded me of how much He loves me just as I am and that there is nothing I could do to earn that unconditional love.

Ephesians 2:4-9 *But God, who is rich in mercy, because of His great love with which He loved us, even when we were dead in trespasses, made us alive together with Christ (by grace you have been saved), and raised us up together, and made us sit together in the heavenly places in Christ Jesus, that in the ages to come He might show the exceeding riches of His grace in His kindness toward us in Christ Jesus. For by grace you have been saved through faith, and that not of yourselves; it is the gift of God, not of works, lest anyone should boast.*

We had been married about one year when it became very clear that if I wanted to have any amount of freedom I would have to trust God to deliver me from my paralyzing fear of driving. Public transportation in Rochester was such that I was very limited as to where I could work or go on my own. When I told my brother Larry about our plans to have John teach me to drive, he exclaimed, "Don't do it, Ronnie! I've known people who got a divorce trying that. It's not a good idea. Pay a professional driving instructor to give you lessons!" I have to admit, there were several times when we thought Larry's advice was not such a bad idea but we persevered.

It was an exercise in faith for both of us. John thought that he would never be able to teach anyone to drive, especially me! He had been driving since he was 16 years old and now had to figure out how to instruct someone else to do something that had become as natural to him as breathing. I was totally clueless about recognizing traffic patterns and for most of my life up to that point enjoyed day dreaming while travelling as a passenger. In other words, I had no idea how to get from A to B in a vehicle. I could tell you what bus or subway or streetcar to take and what stop to get off at and how to go on foot to your destination but to drive there? Forget it!

We owned a standard shift truck at the time so the first thing we did was to purchase a car for me to learn in. We found a nice Ford Taurus and I began studying to obtain my learner's permit. I went over and over the booklet until everyone told me, "Go ahead and take the test already. You don't have to get it perfect!" But to me, nothing less than perfect would do so, when I eventually felt ready, I did get a perfect score. Now it was time to get behind the wheel!

For some inexplicable reason, John had such confidence in my ability that he took me to the Park Avenue area in Rochester at 5 p.m. for my first lesson. We were on a side street and just having him take me there was enough to cause me to say, "Honey, I don't think I am ready yet. Let's try tomorrow."

Chapter 16

I used to say a similar thing to the dentist when I was a little girl. Dr. Hord would be standing over me with drill in hand and say as cheerfully as he could, "Are you ready?"

Of course, I always said, "No, wait a minute." After a while, he stopped asking me that question.

John also ignored my comment and encouraged me in the Lord. "If God can enable me to teach you to drive, He will surely help you to learn. Just have faith! Anyway, I have picked a side street where there is no traffic."

Boy, I thought, *maybe he thinks there is no traffic but I see cars out there.* To my mind, no traffic would be a completely empty road!

We changed seats and I sat behind the wheel. John asked me to turn on the ignition and I just gave him a blank look. "Oh no, you have never turned on the ignition in a car before?" he uttered in amazement. "I would have thought that at some time in your life you might have done that!"

"You don't have to make me feel stupid," I pouted.

"Okay, okay. I'm sorry. I have just never met anyone like you before. Let's be patient and take this slowly, one step at a time. Don't worry. I'm right here beside you." So, I took a deep breath and learned how to turn on the ignition. The next step was to signal and pull out of our parking space but every time I glanced at the side mirror, I saw a car coming or a person riding a bicycle behind me. Even though John told me I had plenty of room and time to pull out, I waited until the road was totally empty before I would do it.

So here I was, driving. Driving until, that is, I came to a four way stop sign. After waving several cars to go ahead, my honey told me that I really had to get to the other side of the street, that he just couldn't keep waving cars on. I froze with fear. He pleaded with me, "Please, just get to the other side of this corner and stop and we can change seats and I will drive us home. You can do this." Well, somehow I managed to follow his instructions and that was the completion of my first lesson.

I thought, *Of all the things I have been through in my life, I have let an inanimate object like a car get the better of me!* I cried out to God to deliver me from such an unreasonable fear. John and I prayed and after accepting advice from our friends, Diane and Buddy, he decided to take me to an empty parking lot for my next lesson. When my sister found out about my driving lessons she declared that my husband was deserving of sainthood for being able to teach me to drive! I enjoyed the parking lot at 15 mph and once I became confident at handling my vehicle I was ready for the road again.

Intersections were a real challenge for me. All the different lines on the road were confusing and I would exclaim as we approached, "What do I do? What do I do?"

John's favorite expression became, "Read the road. You have to learn to read the road!"

Early one Sunday morning, we went out for a spin. Suddenly, John shouted, "Pull over. Pull over!"

"Why?"

"You're driving on the wrong side of the road. Pull over NOW."

"Okay, okay" I muttered as I pulled into a driveway. "But you didn't have to get so excited. There were no cars on the road anyway."

John just took a deep breath and let out a sigh of relief as he gave me an exasperated look. We continued on to the thruway and after some time, he said, "There's a rest stop. Pull in." As I was on the off ramp he said, "Park here." So, I stopped the car. "Not HERE!" he yelled.

"But, you said I should park here. What do you mean?"

"Go, go! Move the car now!" Well, I moved and we found a parking spot and my husband explained to me that we could have been killed if someone had come off the thruway at a high speed while we were just sitting there on the off ramp. "I meant for you to find a parking place in the lot!"

Chapter 16

I replied in my sweetest female voice, "Honey, you really need to be more specific when you give me instructions while I'm driving. I thought you wanted me to stop right where we were."

Later, we came to a toll booth and I was so nervous that I parked too far away to be able to reach the hand of the attendant. Also, I forgot to put my window down, so I banged my hand on the glass as I tried to take the ticket. Next, I pushed the wrong button and the back window went down. Finally, my window was open and the attendant leaned out of her booth as far as she could. As I grabbed hold of the card I said, "Excuse me, I'm a new driver." She was not impressed and neither was my husband!

This reminded me of the first time I went downhill skiing when I shouted, "Excuse me! Excuse me! I'm a new skier," so people could jump out of my way.

The day finally arrived to take my road test and after much prayer I was ready. Thank God, I had a female instructor who was very calm. I even did a parallel park on an incline and the only comment she had when we were finished was, "You need to try not to hit the break so hard when you stop. Congratulations, you passed the test!" I was really relieved because I did not think I could go through taking another test. My legs were shaking so much that I was amazed that I could drive at all. Now, many years later, I can't imagine not being able to drive. What had seemed like an impossible and insurmountable obstacle in my life had been conquered. There truly is nothing that is impossible with God! Also, it was a real victory for John to know that he could teach me to drive, especially the parallel parking. He had been driving a truck for so long that he didn't know if he even remembered how to properly do it himself.

Matthew 19:26 *With men this is impossible, but with God all things are possible.*

While living in Rochester, New York, I developed a serious inner ear infection. It was a particularly cold and snowy winter. I woke up one morning to find that as I began to raise my head off the pillow, the room started spinning around and I had a wave of nausea that propelled me flat on my back. John was working nights and was not home yet. I couldn't move and, quite frankly, I thought I might be having a stroke or something. I had never experienced anything like it before. All kinds of thoughts were attacking my mind, so I set my mind and heart to focus on Jesus while I waited for John to come home.

II Corinthians 10:5 *Casting down arguments and every high thing that exalts itself against the knowledge of God, bringing every thought into captivity to the obedience of Christ.*

John finally arrived to find me immobile on the bed. He called our doctor describing my symptoms. The doctor immediately phoned in a prescription to the drug store for vertigo and told John to give me the pills to steady me so he could bring me into the office.

Later that morning, my husband bundled me up in my green, down-filled parka with a huge furry hood that covered my face making it look like he was carrying a limp rag doll to our car. It turned out that I had a sinus infection which had made its way to my inner ear. I was laid up for several weeks, the first being the most difficult. During that time John created for me what we called our "Oak Forest." We were living in an apartment so he lined up our oak dining room chairs to the kitchen so that I could have something to lean on as I made my way to have a bite to eat and also in the other direction to the bathroom. During that time he had to bathe me. It was a very difficult time for me as I had always been so independent.

When I was able to sit at a table and read again, I slowly read my Bible as long as I could sit up without getting dizzy and the Holy Spirit illuminated specific Scriptures to me.

Chapter 16

> Psalm 118:17 *I shall not die, but live,*
> *And declare the works of the Lord*
>
> Isaiah 42:13 *The LORD shall go forth like a mighty man;*
> *He shall stir up His zeal like a man of war.*
> *He shall cry out, yes, shout aloud;*
> *He shall prevail against His enemies.*

I received a revelation that the Lord's enemies were also my enemies and that He was battling the enemy for me in my weakened state. When I was completely healed, I remember my doctor telling me that he hadn't expected me to get well so quickly as it was one of the worst cases of vertigo that he had seen. It is when we go through trials and feel helpless in our own strength that we can fully understand what it is to lean on and trust in the Lord to deliver us.

About a year later, the vertigo tried to come back and John and I once again visited the Airport church in Toronto. I remember resting on the floor with my eyes closed while Jeremy Sinnot was ministering in music with his guitar. I was thinking how his singing and strumming seemed to be right beside me and when I opened my eyes, there he was. The dizziness left me. As Jeremy sang the songs of the Lord over me, I was healed.

It is interesting how being married will reveal the truth to you about your own character. While John and I were attending Elim Fellowship in Lima, New York, I learned that they had a ministry to students living at the college. I, of course, was excited about it and convinced my darling to accompany me on one of their outreaches.

We were to take a plate of cookies in the early evening hours to a particular student who was a single mom in difficult circumstances and ask her what her needs were. It was in the middle of winter and we were wandering around in almost knee-deep snow in the dark trying to find her residence. All of a sudden, I heard John yell, "Help."

As I turned I saw him disappearing down a hole in the snow. His arm was up in the air holding the plate of cookies and the first words that came out of my mouth were, "Don't drop the cookies!" God bless him, he managed to hold them in the air long enough for me to grab them and then he climbed out.

We finally found our destination and spent a lovely evening praying with the young lady and her children. The thing is, it surprised me that I was more concerned about the cookies than whether my husband had injured himself! When God brings two people together, it is not that you find the perfect person but rather, the perfect mate with all his or her flaws to go through this journey of life together.

I tried not to question John about Viet Nam. I believed that if he wanted to relate any of his experiences to me about his tour of duty, he would do so when he was ready. The following is some of what he has shared with me throughout our marriage.

His basic training was at Fort Carson in Colorado in the winter. He told me that it was so cold that the "Butt Cans" which was what they nicknamed the tin cans for cigarette butts, would freeze over every morning. The barracks were old and probably built during WWII. John's life in the hills had given him excellent physical and mental stamina to be able to endure the rigors of basic training in the high altitude at Fort Carson and later during his tour in Viet Nam.

At basic training he met another fellow from the Buffalo area and they became chums. They used to do a lot of push-ups together as they would often get caught talking when they were not supposed to. This discipline was not difficult for John as he was a country boy and in top physical condition. Apparently, the drill sergeants were pretty decent, and John and the boys had no perception of the horrors that were awaiting them in Viet Nam.

After completing his basic training at Fort Carson, John was sent to Fort Benning in Georgia for Advanced Infantry Training.

Chapter 16

While he was stationed there, his mother and Aunt Wanda came for a surprise visit along with his little sister, Rita. It was a thrill for him. Little did he know that there would only be one more time that he would see his beloved mother. Before John was shipped overseas, he was given a pass to spend a short time at home. His mother died while he was in Viet Nam, and he was given leave to come back for her funeral.

While serving in Viet Nam, John was in the 1st Cavalry Division 2/7 which was General Custer's old outfit. He was stationed at Head Quarters as a radio operator. They maneuvered mostly in teams of two, rotating between base camp and staying out in the field. Actually John said everything was out in the "boonies", the "field." Most of their operations were out of Phan-Thiet, which was on the coast about 90 miles north of Saigon. His unit had the job of going out with the company on first assault on the ground using a PRC25 radio, setting up a 292 antenna for communication back to the base with overhead air support, and forwarding operating elements of the company securing them on "search and destroy" missions. It was truly the grace of God that in more than 20 to 25 first assaults to a landing zone ("LZ") or to a "Hot LZ" they never came under fire. God's miraculous hand of protection was over John as he spent thirteen months in Viet Nam, leaving before the big "Tet Offensive. The Lord brought him safely home to the U.S. in 1967.

A short while after returning home, he attended a little storefront Baptist church in Buffalo where he was shown the love and mercy of Jesus Christ. He surrendered his life to the Lord and was born again, entering into a personal relationship with his Savior.

Romans 10:9-10 That if you confess with your mouth the Lord Jesus and believe in your heart that God has raised Him from the dead, you will be saved. For with the heart one believes unto righteousness, and with the mouth confession is made unto salvation.

When John found employment as a technician with Eastman Kodak in the 1970's, he moved to Rochester, New York. Not long after that the Vietnam War Memorial Mobil Wall came through the area. John's words as he described it to me are: "I went there by myself and just sat down and stared at the wall for a long time. I felt like I was watching a movie about all the men whose names were on that wall as they were dying. Then the Holy Spirit came upon me with a release. The Spirit imparted to me that these men were now in God's hands. Before that, I had been troubled about the whole war, the motives and reasons for being there. I had a lot of unresolved issues and had trouble dealing with it. Now I was able to give it to God and I had peace for the first time since returning home." Even though the Holy Spirit was John's counselor, this shows the healing that can be brought to veterans by having these war memorial walls made available to them.

He then met another Vietnam Veteran while boarding in a rooming house. This fellow invited John to come with him to where some Christians were meeting on Friday nights at Bethel Full Gospel Church. They were Jewish and Gentile believers. Congregation Shema Yisrael was birthed from this small band of worshippers. They later came into possession of their own building at 1326 Winton Road North where they still meet as of this writing. Jonathan Bernis was the rabbi. It was during John's attendance at Shema Yisrael that he was blessed to be able to go on two separate tours to Israel led by Jonathan Bernis. John says that the Bible really came alive for him in the land of Israel. He also participated in a street outreach led by Sid Roth to the Jewish community in New York City in the Brighton Beach area. Later he joined the mission trip to St. Petersburg, Russia where he met me.

>Isaiah 52:7 *How beautiful upon the mountains Are the feet of him who brings good news, Who proclaims peace, Who brings glad tidings of good things, Who proclaims salvation, Who says to Zion, "Your God reigns!"*

CHAPTER 17

"Where's The Fire?"

In 1998, John was downsized from Eastman Kodak. It was as if the rug had been pulled out from under him. He had been living the American dream of working at the same job until retirement and now, at fifty-two years of age, he had to think about learning new skills and starting all over again. The test of our faith comes when life doesn't fit into the neat package that we have envisioned for ourselves. Surrendering to His Will is not always easy, but when we do surrender, we find the perfect peace that only God can give.

Philippians 4:6-8 *Be anxious for nothing, but in everything by prayer and supplication, with thanksgiving, let your requests be made known to God; and the peace of God, which surpasses all understanding, will guard your hearts and minds through Christ Jesus.*

Isaiah 26:3 *You will keep him in perfect peace whose mind is stayed on you because he trusts in you.*

After John lost his job, I had a vivid dream in which we were travelling to Toronto. When we came to what appeared to be the Peace Bridge it looked as if there had been an earthquake or a bomb blast because the bridge was demolished in the center and there were huge rocks overturned in the gorge below. I continue to pray for God to hold back His hand of judgment on the United States and Canada. I pray for His purpose to be fulfilled for this region and for divine protection and peace on our borders.

John sent his resume everywhere but to no avail. He could not find permanent work in the Rochester area, so I had the brilliant idea to move back to Canada! We packed up everything and moved to Toronto during which time we were able to obtain permanent

CHAPTER 17

residency for John. I was ecstatic to be closer to my children and family. I succeeded in landing a few temporary office assignments through an agency, but full-time employment in Toronto was not forthcoming for either of us. However, we were blessed to attend City of David Messianic Congregation with Rabbi Jeff and Janet Forman and visit the Toronto Airport Christian Fellowship during our stay. To top it off, we rented the same apartment from the Freedman's that I had been living in just before we were married!

Finally, John received an offer of employment from a company in Fredonia, New York to which he had previously applied. Since Fredonia was his home town, we packed up again and moved there. That lasted for a while, and then he was laid off again. This time, we packed up and moved to Hamilton, Ontario where we were blessed to attend Metro Church International pastored by Jim and Dianne Paul. Once again, there was no work to be found and it was prudent that we move back to Fredonia as the cost of living in Hamilton was using up all of our resources. As we were discussing our situation, Russ, our previous landlord from Fredonia, telephoned us in Hamilton to let us know that he had an apartment available if we wanted it. We had left him our forwarding address and phone number in case he needed to contact us. We both felt that it was of the Lord that Russ called us like that. What a blessing! We told him we were interested, so he held it for us. We returned in faith, and have been here in Fredonia ever since.

God closed the doors for work in Toronto and Hamilton; but opened doors for employment for both of us in Fredonia. John found work in his field as a maintenance electrician and I as a secretary and then as a teacher's aide. I really enjoyed working with young people and feel that I learned more from them than they did from me. We are both retired now and on a journey of transition once again in this new season of our lives.

Where's The Fire?

In 2003, we drove from Fredonia to Clearwater, Florida to visit John's Aunt Wanda. On the way home having just passed a very small town in Florida, I took my eyes off the road to look at the map, when I felt the vibration of a clunk and a thump under our truck. We had been traveling about 70 mph on the thruway. John had swerved and steered us onto the shoulder of the road to avoid a large object that had suddenly dropped out of the truck in front of us, landing smack in the middle of the road. Once he was able to bring our Ford truck to a stop, he jumped out and saw that one of our dual gas tanks had been punctured. "Grab your purse! Get out of the truck!" John yelled to me. I immediately scrambled out onto the dirt shoulder clutching my handbag. It was pouring rain and it was a miracle that our truck did not ignite.

The driver from the truck up ahead came back to see if we were okay. We hadn't realized that it was the drive shaft from his vehicle that had caused us to go off the road. We thought that he was a Good Samaritan who had stopped to help us. Anyway, he spoke very little English but gave us his cell phone to call 911. As our experience unfolded, it became more and more comical. It reminded me of a movie where two Yankees go down south to find that life is being lived out in slow motion. No one seemed to be in a hurry, not even in an emergency!

It took forever, waiting in the soaking rain, for someone to show up. Finally, a Parks and Recreation policeman arrived to check out the situation. We explained that we needed the fire department because our gas tank had been punctured. He telephoned the Fire Department and then walked ahead to talk with the driver of the truck a little ways up the road. After what seemed like an eternity, he strolled back to us under his huge black umbrella and told us that the driver of the white truck happened to have a spare drive shaft with him and would be on his way. He gave us whatever information he obtained for our insurance company and his police report. Then the policeman and the truck driver ahead of us drove off, leaving us standing there in the pour-

Chapter 17

ing rain. Moments later a fire truck showed up with an extinguisher. Then a tow truck came to take us to the only dealership in town which, thankfully, happened to be Ford.

Of course, this small enterprise did not have a gas tank on hand and had to order one from the state of Georgia. It was while we were staying in the hotel, waiting for our new gas tank to arrive, that I saw on the television that there was a huge power outage in Canada and New York State. Between phone calls to our insurance company, I was calling everyone in my family in Toronto and North Bay to see if they were all right.

It took a few days for the tank to arrive and we were finally on our way again. Thank God, John decided to stop at the gas station to make sure the dealership had filled our new gas tank before we drove home. There I was, relaxing peacefully in the truck when I heard those familiar words again, "Grab your purse! Get out of the truck!" I jumped out and lo and behold, gas was pouring out of the tank as fast as John was putting it in.

I ran to the convenience store to tell the attendant to call the fire department and to put some cones around the area where we were leaking gas. The young man behind the counter seemed to be very sleepy and, in any case, he had no cones. Then, using the store phone, I called the dealership to tell them to come right over. It was almost 5 p.m. so John, thinking that the Ford staff would go home before anyone could come, decided not to wait and to take his chances and drive there. Moments later, a fireman arrived and exclaimed, "Where's the fire?!"

I explained the situation and no sooner had I finished when a man in a tow truck from the Ford dealership screeched into the lot and shouted to me, "Where's the truck?!"

I would say, that was the fastest I had seen anyone move in that town since we had been stuck there. It turned out we had to wait another few days for yet another gas tank and we were finally on our way. We were thankful for God's divine protection and also glad that we were able to sleep in an air conditioned hotel room in Florida instead of a sweltering hot apartment in Fredonia during the blackout.

―――

Psalm 91:11 *For He shall give His angels charge over you, to keep you in all your ways.*

―――

Last year, while praying for healing, I had a vision in which I saw myself as a little child entering the throne room of grace. The Lord was sitting and as I drew near He reached down and picked me up and sat me on His lap. Jesus then pulled a package wrapped with a ribbon around it from behind Him and presented it to me. I immediately knew that it was my gift of healing that He had purchased with His blood.

I believe that He was reminding me of the simplicity of faith. I just need to come to Him as a little child and His grace is sufficient for me.

My authority as a blood bought child of God, a daughter of Abraham, has become a revelation to me once more. The same spirit that raised Jesus from the dead dwells in me to quicken my mortal body and the devil has been a thief and a liar from the beginning! Just as I took back my wallet and bank book from the two thieves in South Africa in 1982, by faith I must take back whatever the enemy has attempted to steal from me.

―――

Romans 8:11 *But if the Spirit of Him who raised Jesus from the dead dwells in you, He who raised Christ from the dead will also give life to your mortal bodies through His Spirit who dwells in you.*

―――

Some months ago, during a church service while I was worshipping the Lord with my hands raised, I had a vision of Jesus above me. His face was covered with a prayer shawl that hung down and the fringes touched the tips of my fingers. I had just been saying to John that morning that I felt like I needed to touch the hem of Jesus' garment like the woman from Luke 8:43-47 who was healed! Oh the mercy of my Messiah to be so attentive to the cry of my heart!

The Scripture that the Lord burned into my heart in 1982, being Romans 12:1-2, has been a strong anchor in my life. *I beseech you therefore, brethren, by the mercies of God, that you present your bodies a living sacrifice, holy, acceptable to God, which is your reasonable service. And do not be conformed to this world, but be transformed by the renewing of your mind, that you may prove what is that good and acceptable and perfect will of God.*

When I meditate on God's word daily, allowing it to transform my heart, it produces life, healing, and joy. When I neglect it and go my own way with my own thoughts and plans, ignoring the grace of God in my life, I produce heartache, disappointment, and pain. I have eternal gratitude for the unfathomable grace and faithfulness of God in my life!

>I Corinthians 1:9 *God is faithful, by whom you were called into the fellowship of His Son, Jesus Christ our Lord.*

Instead of discarding this scarred and shattered life, the Lord has gently taken me into His hands to create a new vessel fit for the Master's use. He has not only restored me, He has given me a new heart and a new life in Him. There is nothing that this world has to offer that can compare to even one moment in His Presence. There is nothing that can satisfy a hungry soul but the Son of God Himself!

>Jeremiah 18:1-6 *The word which came to Jeremiah from the LORD, saying: "Arise and go down to the potter's house, and there I will cause you to hear My words." Then I went down to the potter's house, and there he was, making something at the wheel. And the vessel that he made of clay was marred in the hand of the potter; so he made it again into another vessel, as it seemed good to the potter to make. Then the word of the LORD came to me, saying: "O house of Israel, can I not do with you as this potter?" says the LORD. "Look, as the clay is in the potter's hand, so are you in My hand, O house of Israel!"*

Ezekiel 36:26 *I will give you a new heart and put a new spirit within you; I will take the heart of stone out of your flesh and give you a heart of flesh.*

I cannot say that I have always been obedient to the Lord since I was born again in 1982. Walking with the Lord does not mean that I have already attained perfection.

Philippians 3:14 *I press toward the goal for the prize of the upward call of God in Christ Jesus.*

Following Jesus is not a matter of using my own strength to keep from doing wrong, but rather a revelation of the love and mercy of God in an intimate relationship with Him that causes me to desire the things of the Kingdom and not the things of this world. I cannot change the past but, because of His loving kindness, His forgiveness and His mercy, I can trust my Heavenly Father with my future as I continue to surrender my hopes, my plans and my dreams to Him.

Matthew 6:33 *But seek first the Kingdom of God, and His righteousness; and all these things shall be added to you.*

Whenever I feel that I have failed, or that my life is of no significance, the Holy Spirit brings this to my remembrance. The Lord promises to complete that which He has begun in me.

Philippians 1:6 *Being confident of this very thing, that he who has begun a good work in you will complete it until the day of Jesus Christ.*

It happened that I was struggling with feelings of failure recently. That particular Sunday in church, I asked for prayer for physical healing. The lady, Pat, who was praying for me did not know anything about what was going on in my heart or what was happening in my life at the time. While she was praying for my physical healing, she said, *"Rhonda, I keep hearing the Lord say that He is very pleased with your life. He is very pleased with your life."* She repeated it twice. She went on, *"Just continue to do what you are doing and He will take care of the rest."* I stand

Chapter 17

amazed once again at Abba Father's faithfulness to me; His all-consuming love for me; for not giving up on me. He zoomed right into my heart by putting words in Pat's mouth that were exactly what I needed to hear at that moment. The last thing that I expected to hear that day was that Father God was pleased with my life. It is so much in our human nature to think that we have to make ourselves perfect before we will be accepted or loved by God. He knows the longings of our innermost being, and all we have to do is to come to Him with a sincere heart.

When I surrendered my heart to Jesus in 1982, the aching emptiness was finally filled. He had been waiting for me with arms open wide to embrace me with His immeasurable, all-consuming love, and though my sins were like crimson, He made me as white as snow (I John 1:7, Isaiah 1:18).

II Corinthians 5:17 *Therefore, if anyone is in Christ, he is a new creation; old things have passed away; behold, all things have become new.*

I can do nothing without God's grace and power in my life. As Jesus hung on the cross and cried, *"Father forgive them for they know not what they do"* (Luke 23:34), He was the embodiment of grace. He hung on that cross for me. His grace is personal. But He is no longer on the cross. He has risen and now is seated at the right hand of the Father, interceding for me (Romans 8:34)! My desire is to be more and more like Jesus so that I can be a reflection of Him to a lost and dying world. I seek to know Him in His fullness, His holiness, His goodness, His faithfulness and to gaze upon His Glory.

John and I are two people who, in man's eyes, did not appear to be likely candidates to be joined in marriage. But our Heavenly Father was weaving a tapestry of our individual lives that were to be intertwined in His perfect timing. We find ourselves to be compatible in the simple things of life. We love to spend time whenever we can with our children and grandchildren. We enjoy being together on a cold winters' night listening to the wind howling outside, watching the snow landing in blotches on our windows. I take pleasure in strolling through the woods with John as he points out the different species of trees to me. More than anything, we love to talk about the goodness of God and to pray together. Most importantly, we have a singleness of purpose to seek and know the Lord more and more intimately.

John is not only my husband but my best friend. God has poured out so much grace on our marriage. Where I have areas of weakness, John is strong and where he has areas of weakness, I am strong. John has come to love our children and grandchildren as his own as God has created a father's heart in him.

We consider the challenges and trials in our lives to be very small in comparison to the big God that we serve. When we surrender our hurts and our pains to the God of love and mercy, He heals us so completely that we are then able to have compassion on others who are hurting. It is truly the goodness of God that leads us to repentance. Romans 2:4 *Or do you despise the riches of His goodness, forbearance, and longsuffering, not knowing that the goodness of God leads you to repentance?* One story John likes to tell is how the first time I gave him a hug, he was set free from depression. He said that he experienced a supernatural love that just drove it out. It was during my first visit to him in the United States while we were strolling through the village of Arcade where we had gone for ice cream. For some reason, I cannot remember that hug. I do remember the ice cream. I guess the ice cream was more important to me at the time!

> Proverbs 3:5-7 *Trust in the LORD with all your heart, And lean not on your own understanding; In all your ways acknowledge Him, And He shall direct your paths. Do not be wise in your own eyes; Fear the LORD and depart from evil.*

Chapter 17

John and I don't know what our next step is to be but one thing we do know is that we were brought together for God's purpose and as we seek His face He will show us the way that we should go. So for now, we say, "Hineni, Lord," which is Hebrew for "Here am I." We wait for Him as the bride longingly awaits her bridegroom. We look forward to that day when we will be changed in the twinkling of an eye and we will see Him as He is and be made like Him.

> I John 3:2-3 *Beloved, now we are children of God; and it has not yet been revealed what we shall be, but we know that when He is revealed, we shall be like Him, for we shall see Him as He is. And everyone who has this hope in Him purifies himself, just as He is pure.*

> John 17:3 *And this is eternal life, that they may know You, the only true God, and Jesus Christ whom You have sent.*

My prayer for you, my reader, is *that He would grant you, according to the riches of His glory, to be strengthened with might through His Spirit in the inner man, that Christ may dwell in your hearts through faith; that you, being rooted and grounded in love, may be able to comprehend with all the saints what is the width and length and depth and height— to know the love of Christ which passes knowledge; that you may be filled with all the fullness of God* (Ephesians 3:16-19).

May you have a burning desire to study the Word of God and as you diligently study, may the precious Holy Spirit reveal Jesus to you. May you cherish God's Word as a precious jewel and come to understand that the most magnificent love story ever written is for you. As you are transformed into the likeness of Jesus, may you be a shining light in a dark world so that the lost, the hurting, the sick, and the dying will be drawn to Him, the light of the world, through you. John 1:1 *In the beginning was the Word, and the Word was with God, and the Word was God.* To know God's Word is to know Him and to know Him is everything!

It is my prayer that this account of my life has exalted and magnified Jesus. He has taken the pain and turned it into joy. He has broken the curse and turned it into blessing so that I do not see myself as having suffered but as having been blessed by God. I pray that you, my reader, will have an encounter with the living God and be ignited and inspired to follow Jesus to the finish line. May He become your magnificent obsession.

Let Jesus Come In

Let Jesus come into your heart
Even though you're far apart
He came to die that you might live
For you His life He freely gives

Let Him reach into your soul
He was broken
To make you whole

Let Jesus come in
Let Jesus come in

When you cry out
And no man hears
Have no doubt
For He is near
Your soul cries out
And no man hears

Let Jesus come in
Let Jesus come in

Rhonda Lea, 1992

Appendix

ENCOURAGING SCRIPTURES

1 Corinthians 15:47-57

The first man was of the earth, made of dust; the second Man is the Lord from heaven. As was the man of dust, so also are those who are made of dust; and as is the heavenly Man, so also are those who are heavenly. And as we have borne the image of the man of dust, we shall also bear the image of the heavenly Man. Now this I say, brethren, that flesh and blood cannot inherit the kingdom of God; nor does corruption inherit incorruption. Behold, I tell you a mystery: We shall not all sleep, but we shall all be changed—in a moment, in the twinkling of an eye, at the last trumpet. For the trumpet will sound, and the dead will be raised incorruptible, and we shall be changed. For this corruptible must put on incorruption, and this mortal must put on immortality. So when this corruptible has put on incorruption, and this mortal has put on immortality, then shall be brought to pass the saying that is written:

"Death is swallowed up in victory."

"O Death, where is your sting?

O Hades, where is your victory?"

The sting of death is sin, and the strength of sin is the law. But thanks be to God, who gives us the victory through our Lord Jesus Christ.

Romans 6:13-14

And do not present your members as instruments of unrighteousness to sin, but present yourselves to God as being alive from the dead, and your members as instruments of righteousness to God. For sin shall not have dominion over you, for you are not under law but under grace.

1 John 1:9

If we confess our sins, He is faithful and just to forgive us our sins and to cleanse us from all unrighteousness.

1 John 3:2-3

Beloved, now we are children of God; and it has not yet been revealed what we shall be, but we know that when He is revealed, we shall be like Him, for we shall see Him as He is. And everyone who has this hope in Him purifies himself, just as He is pure.

SOME MESSIANIC PROPHECIES AND FULFILLMENTS

Micah 5:2 Prophecy
But you, Bethlehem Ephrathah,
Though you are little among the thousands of Judah,
Yet out of you shall come forth to Me
The One to be Ruler in Israel,
Whose goings forth are from of old,
From everlasting.

Matthew 2:1-5 Fulfillment
Now after Jesus was born in Bethlehem of Judea in the days of Herod the king, behold, wise men from the East came to Jerusalem, saying, "Where is He who has been born King of the Jews? For we have seen His star in the East and have come to worship Him."

When Herod the king heard this, he was troubled, and all Jerusalem with him. And when he had gathered all the chief priests and scribes of the people together, he inquired of them where the Christ was to be born.

So they said to him, "In Bethlehem of Judea, for thus it is written by the prophet:…"

Zechariah 12:9-10 Prophecy
It shall be in that day that I will seek to destroy all the nations that come against Jerusalem. And I will pour on the house of David and on the inhabitants of Jerusalem the Spirit of grace and supplication; then they will look on Me whom they pierced. Yes, they will mourn for Him as one mourns for his only son, and grieve for Him as one grieves for a firstborn.

Revelation 1:7 Future fulfillment
Behold, He is coming with clouds, and every eye will see Him, even they who pierced Him. And all the tribes of the earth will mourn because of Him. Even so, Amen.

Zechariah 9:9 Prophecy
Rejoice greatly, O daughter of Zion!
Shout, O daughter of Jerusalem!
Behold, your King is coming to you;
He is just and having salvation,
Lowly and riding on a donkey,
A colt, the foal of a donkey.

John 12:12-15 Fulfillment
The next day a great multitude that had come to the feast, when they heard that Jesus was coming to Jerusalem, took branches of palm trees and went out to meet Him, and cried out: "Hosanna! Blessed is He who comes in the name of the LORD! The King of Israel!"

Then Jesus, when He had found a young donkey, sat on it; as it is written: "Fear not, daughter of Zion; Behold, your King is coming, Sitting on a donkey's colt."

Deuteronomy 18:15,17-19 Prophecy
The LORD your God will raise up for you a Prophet like me from your midst, from your brethren. Him you shall hear, ...

And the LORD said to me: "What they have spoken is good. I will raise up for them a Prophet like you from among their brethren, and will put My words in His mouth, and He shall speak to them all that I command Him. And it shall be that whoever will not hear My words, which He speaks in My name, I will require it of him."

Acts 3:22-26 Fulfillment
"For Moses truly said to the fathers, 'The Lord your God will raise up for you a Prophet like me from your brethren. Him you shall hear in all things, whatever He says to you. 23 And it shall be that every soul who will not hear that Prophet shall be utterly destroyed from among the people.' 24 Yes, and all the prophets, from Samuel and those who follow, as many as have spoken, have also foretold these days. 25 You are sons of the prophets, and of the covenant which God made with our fathers, saying to Abraham, 'And in your seed all the families of the earth shall be blessed.' 26 To you first, God, having raised up His Servant Jesus, sent Him to bless you, in turning away every one of you from your iniquities."

John 5:39-47 Jesus' Words
You search the Scriptures, for in them you think you have eternal life; and these are they which testify of Me. But you are not willing to come to Me that you may have life. ... I have come in My Father's name, and you do not receive Me; if another comes in his own name, him you will receive. ... Do not think that I shall accuse you to the Father; there is one who accuses you—Moses, in whom you trust. For if you believed Moses, you would believe Me; for he wrote about Me. But if you do not believe his writings, how will you believe My words?

Isaiah 53 Prophecy
Who has believed our report?
And to whom has the arm of the Lord been revealed?
For He shall grow up before Him as a tender plant,
And as a root out of dry ground.
He has no form or comeliness;
And when we see Him,
There is no beauty that we should desire Him.
He is despised and rejected by men,
A Man of sorrows and acquainted with grief.
And we hid, as it were, our faces from Him;
He was despised, and we did not esteem him.

Surely He has borne our griefs
And carried our sorrows;
Yet we esteemed Him stricken,
Smitten by God, and afflicted.
But He was wounded for our transgressions,
He was bruised for our inquities;
The chastisement for our peace was upon Him,
And by His stripes we are healed.
All we like sheep have gone astray;
We have turned, every one, to his own way;
And the Lord has laid on Him the iniquity of us all.
He was oppressed and He was afflicted,
Yet He opened not His mouth;

*He was led as a lamb to the slaughter,
And as a sheep before its shearers is silent,
So He opened not his mouth.*

*He was taken from prison and from judgment,
And who will declare His generation?
For He was cut off from the land of the living;
For the transgressions of My people He was stricken.
And they made His grave with the wicked—
 But with the rich at His death,
Because He had done no violence,
Nor was any deceit in His mouth.*

*Yet it pleased the Lord to bruise Him;
He has put Him to grief.
When You make His soul an offering for sin,
He shall see His seed, He shall prolong His days,
And the pleasure of the Lord shall prosper in His hand.
He shall see the travail of His soul, and be satisfied.
By His knowledge My righteous Servant shall justify many,
For He shall bear their iniquities.
Therefore I will divide Him a portion with the great,
And He shall divide the spoil with the strong,
Because He poured out His soul unto death,
And He was numbered with the transgressors,
And He bore the sin of many,
And made intercession for the transgressors.*

Ezekiel 18:30-32 Prophecy

"Therefore I will judge you, O house of Israel, every one according to his ways," says the Lord GOD. "Repent, and turn from all your transgressions, so that iniquity will not be your ruin. Cast away from you all the transgressions which you have committed, and get yourselves a new heart and a new spirit. For why should you die, O house of Israel? For I have no pleasure in the death of one who dies," says the Lord GOD. "Therefore turn and live!"

This Book Is Available At:

olivepresspublisher.com

amazon.com

barnesandnoble.com

etc.

BOOK STORE MANAGERS may obtain this book at 40% discount, returnable, through

Olive Press Publisher

by e-mailing: olivepressbooks@gmail.com

or also 40%, returnable through

Ingram Book Company

www.ingramcontent.com/pod-product-compliance
Lightning Source LLC
Chambersburg PA
CBHW071308110426
42743CB00042B/1217